22

A GUIDE
FOR YOUNG
ATHLETES

22

A GUIDE FOR YOUNG ATHLETES

BUILT BY ATHLETES. FOR ATHLETES.

ANDREW NELSON

© 2024 by Andrew Nelson

All rights reserved. This book or any portion thereof may not be reproduced or used in any manner whatsoever without the express written permission of the publisher except for the use of brief quotations in a book review.

Lake Elmo Publishing

ISBN: 979-8-9906948-0-4

For more information about *22—The Guide for Young Athletes*, the TM22 Athlete Alliance, or ongoing research and resources for athletes, visit tm22athletes.com.

In memory and honor of Todd Mann, #22.

Thank you for showing me the power of believing in a young athlete.

"Courage, hard work, self-mastery, and intelligent effort are all essential to successful life."
—Theodore Roosevelt

CONTENTS

Preface		xi
Introduction: The Young-Athlete Mountain		xiii
Chapter 1:	The Life of a Young Athlete	1
Chapter 2:	TM22 Part I	15
Chapter 3:	In Pursuit of Success	25
Chapter 4:	Tracking Former Athletes—Research, Data, and Advice	39
Chapter 5:	The Athlete Outpost—Key Skills and Lessons Critical to Your Quest	55
Chapter 6:	The Final Ascent	97
Chapter 7:	Understanding and Utilizing an Important Ally—the Adults	119
Chapter 8:	The Young Athlete Den—Models, Formulas, and Tools	141
Chapter 9:	Mastering the Art of Being a Young Athlete	191
Chapter 10:	The Land Beyond the Mountain	203
Conclusion: TM22 Part II		227
Afterword		243
Acknowledgments and Gratitude		249
About the Author		253
References and Additional Resources		255

PREFACE

This guide is designed for the young athlete on a quest for greatness, in athletics and in life.

Built by athletes for athletes, together we form a team that will learn to define our own success and create a path to achieve it. This alliance will allow us to acquire advice from athletes that have come before us, equip ourselves with important skills that will help set us apart, and learn how to make your experiences as an athlete benefit you on any path you choose.

If you want to make all the sacrifice and time you're putting in worth it, reach your maximum potential on and off the field, and leave behind a legacy you're proud of, this book is for you.

INTRODUCTION: THE YOUNG-ATHLETE MOUNTAIN

When you choose to become an athlete, you join other athletes at the base of a mountain.

This mysterious, metaphorical mountain in front of you symbolizes the life of a young athlete and the difficult journey ahead. Far above the clouds awaits the summit—a place that represents accomplishing your goals, reaching your full potential, and exceeding all expectations. This mountain is full of obstacles, sacrifice, and hard work, and you will only get one chance to climb it. Equipped with your own unique set of skills, strengths, and inner purpose, you set off on a path never traveled, never to be traveled again. This is your path, your journey, your story.

No matter the size or how unfair an obstacle along your path may seem, you will have to find a way to overcome it. There are no shortcuts. Excuses aren't welcome. Progress must be earned. This mountain owes you nothing. You will be accountable for the footprints you leave behind.

Never again will you have as great an opportunity to set yourself apart and prepare yourself for the journeys ahead. It won't be easy, but you have done right by choosing it. Along the way, you will need to learn to embrace difficult times, adapt so that you can weather any type of storm, and keep moving forward no matter what the terrain.

This alliance with adversity will be your opportunity to discover and show your true character, create the legacy you wish to leave behind, and discover the answers to some difficult questions deep within. Why is being an athlete important to me? What sacrifices am I willing to make to set myself apart from the other athletes standing next to me? What is my own definition of success, as an athlete and in life? What does it take to get to the next level, and how bad do I want it? Is all the time, hard work, energy, and pressure being put on me by others worth it? How do I want to be remembered as an athlete, and what principles do I stand for? These are just a few of the important questions this journey will help you answer.

The goal isn't to conquer this mountain, and everyone's mountain is different. If you wish to one day become the best version of yourself and be at peace with your time as an athlete, hold yourself accountable and pay attention to the lessons and perspective this journey can provide.

Why 22? What is TM22?

TM22 began as the initials of a man and is now also a symbol, an alliance, a way of life, an approach. This guide contains lessons, research, advice, and tools carefully selected to show you how to reach high levels of success in sports and in the life that follows. The TM22 model is about putting more control in the hands of athletes and providing them with the tools needed along the way, regardless of the challenge or choices that need to be made.

The number 22 holds power of its own. Some believe it's a sign of good luck or of positive things to come. I will explain how it may help you "manifest your destiny" later in this book.

Why should you read this book?

This book is designed to help you succeed regardless of skill level, experience, or the system you're in. Regardless of obstacles, a bad coach, parents, or a global pandemic, there are things you can do to maximize your time as an athlete and make all the time, energy, and sacrifice worth it. This is your one-and-only chance to be a young athlete; how you navigate this path and your ability to acquire important skills along the way could impact your trajectory in life. Your time as a young athlete won't last long; it's important you make the most of it and learn quickly from those that came before you. This book will shed light on the components and the paths that have set the elite athletes apart from others and can do the same for you.

Who should read this book?

This book was built by athletes, for athletes, but it really should be read by anyone who has any level of involvement with a young athlete. Coaches, teachers, parents, athletic directors, and mentors join young athletes on this team, and each plays an important role. Winning championships, setting records, getting scholarships, and exceeding expectations can all be part of the to-do list, but your integrity doesn't have to be sacrificed along the way. If you wish to be spoken of as an athlete who accomplished great things, reached his or her maximum potential, and will be a respected athlete who people will remember for all the right reasons, this is a tool that can help you do that.

This book is designed for the athlete who wants to be a great athlete and a great human—you don't have to choose—and the pursuit of one can help the other. If you're a young reader or reading just isn't really your thing, some of the concepts in this book may feel like a stretch. This stretch is by design. Do I think every athlete could benefit from reading this book? Yes, but I've designed it for athletes who want to be challenged, not coddled.

How is this book organized?

The book follows a strategic progression that aims to provide the proper foundation for athletes to gain perspective, equip themselves with the right tools, and leave them empowered to know how to make the decisions needed to excel. This book isn't attempting to provide a shortcut; lessons can be learned from making mistakes, but it is important to streamline information and learn from those that came before us so it can be used during the window when you need it.

This book was designed to help athletes create the right systems and habits needed to have a *sustained* impact, not a one-time blast of motivation. This approach can help you navigate your way through the latest buzzwords, expensive showcases, a bad coach, lots of distractions, and a rapidly changing young athlete landscape. I have compiled decades of personal experience as an athlete and coach, gathered input and advice from former and current athletes, coaches, teachers, or parents, and shared all of this in a format that doesn't depend on anyone other than the athlete holding the book. This book is designed to be thought-provoking, meaning it will try to encourage you to think about your own story, ask questions, and grow from this process.

Who is this book about?

This book is about you and your current quest, but it's also designed for the person you will someday be after your days of being an athlete are over. You are responsible for deciding who you want to be and determining the path to get there. As you flip through the pages, you should apply everything you read to your own personal journey. Think often about your own experiences, lessons, and the legacy you are writing by your daily actions and choices.

As a young athlete, I wanted nothing more than to reach the top and make others proud. It was this mindset that sent me on a journey containing many ups and downs, some of which nearly took my life. I'm not a sports psychologist or a professional athlete, but I am a teacher and a coach, and I know how important this part of your life can be. I know the impact it can have beyond just sports, and I know why doing it the right way matters. This guide includes limited amounts of my own personal stories and examples of other athletes in part to encourage you not to compare your journey to that of others but also to get you information in the most direct way possible. For more stories, interviews, and examples, visit the TM22 athlete website.

How do I use this book?

You decide. Read it, write in it, cross things out, question things, add things, take your favorite quotes and write them in your journal, sweat on it, give it to a friend, and make your parents and coaches read it. This book, like life, will be what you make it. Use this book to challenge yourself just as you would in the weight room, at practice, or on the field.

This book is just a tool. Use the models to help you understand your own quest and see the big picture. You need to develop your own perspective, learn your own lessons, and determine your own principles to live by. Its power will be up to you to determine. This is a unique tool designed for athletes willing to do the work, not someone looking for a shortcut or the easiest path.

Why now?
The best athletes are relentless learners. Studying the lives and habits of former athletes and our pursuit of finding ways to reach our maximum potential should be ongoing, but it's a pivotal time for athletes and the evolving environment being created for future athletes. There are athletes in need now (you), and together we can make an impact on recalibrating the trajectory of sports. There are lots of former athletes that have already gone through a lot of what athletes are going through now, have great advice, and want to genuinely help others avoid having the same regrets and not miss out on the magic. This book allows us to get on the same page and serves as a foundation to build from. Athletes are stronger together; this book aims to create that bridge.

Why not you?
The world rewards those willing to do the work, so why not you? Use this book to learn from other athletes who have come before you and apply it to your own quest. You may not know what the destination looks like yet, but you already knew at an early age that it doesn't really matter—it's the direction of your dreams that drives you and what you overcome to get there that will write your story. You're not alone; your journey matters; it's up to you to determine who you want to be and do the work needed to get there. Before we continue any further down this path, it's important to shed light on the current life of the young athlete, how we got here, and why it's important to understand what comes next.

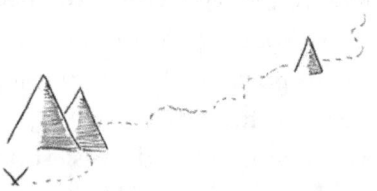

1

THE LIFE OF A YOUNG ATHLETE

No one knows the journey that you're on, how it looks, or how it feels—except you.

You and I are just a couple of the 100+ billion other humans who have lived on our planet throughout time, but only one has ever spent a day in your shoes. You are the only one who can see what's happening on the outside and the inside—both equally important. While the challenges today's athletes face include both old and new, there's a lot that all athletes can relate to and always will. This includes your biggest rival and even those young athletes on the same quest thousands of years ago. Imagine if you looked closely at what their lives were like and what they went through and applied that perspective to your own quest. The best athletes do.

If you want to reach your maximum potential, you must be willing to adapt, blaze new trails, and learn selectively from those who came before you. The good news: you're not alone, and it's up to you to determine where and how your journey as a young athlete will end.

The following chapter will look closer at the evolving lives of young athletes, discuss why this path is so important in athletics and beyond, and ask some questions that help us identify who it is that's reading this book and why our paths have now crossed.

The Definition of a Young Athlete

This book focuses on those involved with some level of sports within the age range of eight to twenty-two. Of course, there are a lot of things that happen in the lives of the athletes on the outside of this spectrum, but the entrance to being a young athlete, from intermediate to high school to the college window, and transitions within are particularly critical. Skill levels and abilities aren't important at this point; this guide is designed for the athlete and person you intend to become.

The Evolution of a Young-Athlete Life

There are a lot of variables that determine what the life of a young athlete looks like: the athlete, family, location, culture, time of year you were born, period in history, opportunity, gender, money, genetics, school, habits, and the adults you're surrounded by—the list goes on. This makes it difficult to explain what it's like for any one athlete, but we can make some basic assumptions.

We know that for even the earliest athletes, this is a period of life that involves growing bodies, increasing amounts of responsibility, future-altering choices and decisions, the creation of relationships that can last a lifetime, and varying levels of adversity, struggle, and failure. There is no other time in your life where there will be this many new, important challenges and decisions that need to be made, with varied levels of perspective to make them. It's these same reasons that also make it so memorable. So why do we care about what other athletes are going through, especially those from thousands of years ago? A lot of what's happening "on the inside" is still the same. It's how we're wired. There are lessons we can learn and mistakes we can avoid, and it's important to again note: you're not alone. What it means to be a young athlete can and should continue to evolve, but it should evolve with the best interest of athletes in mind.

A Long Time Ago...

The first young athletes may have been some of the earliest humans. These hunter-gatherers were playing a sport called survival. The team—family. The game plan—don't die. Entire lifetimes were spent training, learning from their elders, and working together to complete the daily missions. Different stakes. Different players. Same path. We are here today because those young athletes long ago succeeded in helping their teams (families) survive. We are all descendants of the athletes in those tribes. Being able to overcome adversity is in our DNA.

Over the course of hundreds of thousands of years, modern humans have continued to evolve both inside and out. Whether it was surviving multiple ice ages, the introduction of fire, agriculture, civilizations, the ability to communicate ideas, or some other obstacle, there soon became more time, energy, and brain capacity available to think about things other than just survival. Examples would be things that entertain us, ways to communicate ideas, the future, or even activities that better prepare us for war. "Better" food and more of it also allowed for more growth, better health, and stronger humans. Across the world, people started to develop a wide range of physical competitions, first wrestling, then throwing objects, and then some humans started to experiment with sports that involved both. In many cases the first team sports became the perfect training for armies, requiring physically fit humans who had the ability to work together. (In genetic terms, this really isn't a lot of time for any drastic changes to occur to our DNA and we should feel good knowing that all we need is already inside of all of us.)

In 2014, I traveled with a group of teachers to Rapa Nui (Easter Island). While there we visited Orongo, the home of the ancient Birdman Competition. This competition occurred hundreds of years ago and, to summarize, required competitors to scale down the edge of a cliff nearly a thousand feet high, swim across a section of the ocean while avoiding sharks (and drowning), climb another rock hundreds of feet high, steal a bird egg from the nest at the top, carry the egg safely back across the ocean with a strap across their foreheads, and bring it back up the cliff to where they began. Young athletes were training and competing in one of the most remote, untouched places on the planet. Events like these were happening across the globe. There were periods where the growth of sports and the population of athletes that played them would be interrupted by major global events, but it would only be temporary.

It's important to understand where we came from, how we got here, and why. Over time there have also been things that haven't changed. For example, we still have the need to acquire new skills and knowledge from those who came before us, the need for proper training and health, the importance of working together to reach a common goal, and for some an unwavering inner desire to succeed on and off the field. Our world has changed, and humans have changed, but the intentional thread of what makes being a successful young athlete so important remains.

A key component to identify here and protect is *the importance of struggle*. This struggle is what forces growth and the need to adapt. I'm not proposing we need to seek new ways to create struggle, but it's important to understand why the struggle is not just ok but is good for you. You have the skills and toughness and drive inside of you to not just overcome but thrive and feel better having worked through it. The best things in life are often the things that are hard and the things you're responsible for, not what's easy or provide instant gratification. This book aims to help athletes embrace and have the tools needed to take advantage of the struggle.

Present Day

Playing sports and the lessons they can teach have never been so important, but a lot has changed over the past fifty years. We have seen the rapid influence of technology, advancements in equipment, the arrival of things called transfer portals and name-image-likeness contracts, a better understanding of training and nutrition, and an onslaught of mind-altering distractions. Most athletes don't know a life without instant connectivity, and there is no turning back.

Growing numbers of opportunities (for some), instant accessibility to infinite information, a new market for people to make money, and improvement to communication methods have allowed for youth sports to explode on a global scale—and with it a brand-new set of challenges. Some of which include varying levels of pressure from parents and coaches, technology-driven distractions (e.g., social media), the struggle to find a "healthy" dynamic balance between school/athletics/life, overuse of developing muscles, premature assessment of future potential, mental/emotional burnout via early single-sport specialization and forgetting what makes being a young athlete so important and skills it teaches. Perhaps most important is our current definition (or disappearance of definition) of success for today's athletes.

It's important to note here that all the new challenges are not just being put on young athletes but on the adults involved with this quest as well. Everyone on the young athlete's team needs to take ownership of the factors within their control and understand the role they play. There are some who think there are too many choices, too many opportunities for their kids to choose from, and they are now spread too thin, while others don't have the luxury of having any of these options and limited access. The purpose of this book is not to debate who's got it worse but to agree that everyone has obstacles to overcome; the young-athlete mountain has changed a great deal and will continue to do so. Change is a good thing; the challenges I listed will look a lot different in just ten years. It's not to be feared, but it's important to understand how it all began, be aware of current trends, and use this knowledge to adapt to a rapidly changing way of life.

Tip: Just because something is a certain way right now doesn't mean it will always be, good or bad. If your habits haven't been the best in the past, or you've had a bad month, these can and will change. Take control of changes you want to see—habits, attitude, perspective, or hard work. The best athletes not only embrace change but also take advantage of something most fear.

Looking Ahead

When I was a kid, I remember seeing a book on my dad's bookshelf called *An Incomplete Guide to the Future* by Willis Harman. I thought I had discovered the most valuable artifact known to man, which could give me all the answers I'd ever need. Willis

Harman was a professor of future studies. He looked closely at the futures of various systems and analyzed patterns, trends, general assumptions, who is involved, and how today's actions are impacting the future, etc., all to map out potential scenarios shedding light on the next paradigm. In his words, his work was intended "to explore how our vision of the future affects the crucial decisions of today." We are attempting to do something similar here, and we need current athletes to look out for their successors.

We don't know all the challenges that future athletes will face, but we can, however, begin to look at the signs and begin to forecast carefully. The influence of technology, the learning capabilities, and pedagogical strategies used by teachers in schools, which groups are gaining/losing opportunities and why, the impact of our parenting styles, different amounts of experience and tools to handle anxiety and adversity, the rapid growth of the amount of "elite" travel teams at younger and younger ages, online- and AI-training tools, lack of funding in schools to sustain athletic programs, the loss of amateurism, increased parental influence on coaches, the sterilization of sports, the age of transfers, pressure to "grow your brand," a decrease in good mentors willing to coach and officiate are just a few of the factors that should be on our radar. There will also be challenges that seem absurd to even consider and hard to predict, such as a global pandemic. The good news, if there is any group that is used to overcoming challenges and using adversity to their advantage, it's those that have chosen the path of being a young athlete.

Regardless of the rapidly changing factors, both known and unknown, we must remember what makes playing sports so great and the lessons that can be learned as a young athlete. What if we used athletics to create tough, resilient, principle-led young people equipped with decision-making skills? Important note: we don't need to sacrifice anything about being elite to do this.

Why Is the Life of a Young Athlete so Important?

The importance of the well-being of athletes reaches far beyond just the ones holding this book, sports, the lives of young people, or those that have any connection to youth or athletics.

In the next fifty years, we, as a planet, are going to have to overcome a myriad of new challenges. We will be dependent upon this generation, many of whom are today's young athletes, to decide the paths chosen and to carry us forward on them. In the not-so-distant future, many of the jobs we know today will either be different, automated, or not exist anymore. Our health care system is being impacted heavily by the number of health problems related to a lack of movement, exercise, and good health practices. We're witnessing more civil discourse and a lack of empathy for our fellow humans. Athletes are quitting at earlier ages or opting to not even sign up at all. Just the fact that there are so many "other things" to do that don't require as much money, cause less stress, and provide gratification quicker are factors worth noting. The list could go on, but this is a book about athletes and solutions, not problems and excuses. The future we are creating is going to require a culture of excellence with character, athletes with a new set of skills, and even a new mindset. This army of today's young people needs to be tough and capable of overcoming adversity, handling pressure, making sound decisions, offering a willingness to be accountable for their actions, having the ability to regulate their emotions and manage anxiety, and avoiding an onslaught of new distractions.

The good news is that competition helps us learn about ourselves, our strengths, weaknesses, how to overcome anxiety, and learn important life lessons. Sports are the perfect place for a positive relationship between the young and old to occur. We live in a world that at times struggles to embrace diversity; there is no better place than youth athletics (and professional sports) to teach the importance of being open minded and valuing those things that make us different. In youth sports, it is common to have teams of both boys and girls, black and white, big and small, fast, and slow, and they all respect each other as they work toward a common goal. This lesson of empathy is critical and shows why equal opportunities for all are a must moving forward. It's the type of athletes willing to read a book like this that can help continue to steward the path of young athletes and continue these important things and why I'm including it here.

Don't underestimate the importance of your current path and how you choose to travel it.

The Power of Sports in Acquiring Decision-Making Skills

I'm a believer in the important role decision-making skills play in life and our ability to get better at it. Sports is the perfect environment to gain that experience (if we allow it to), and it can have lifelong impacts, so it's important it's done right. Which sports you choose to play, who your friends are, how you spend your time, how you deal with a coach or boss you don't agree with, how to respond to adversity, these are some early choices that have long-term impacts.

The target audience chosen for this book also happens to be when some of the most lasting, impactful memories occur. It is also when some of the most important decisions need to be made. Compared to just one hundred years ago, the number of options available and types of choices today's youth must make are incredible—navigating social media, the arrival of transfer portals, Name-Image-Likeness (NIL) agreements, club teams, knowing the difference between good and bad advice, and who to trust, etc. At an early age, we have instincts but lack the training or perspective to make life-impacting decisions on our own. Mentors, teachers, coaches, and parents willing to help do what is best for the athlete are critical. Learning "how" to think, gaining experience making decisions, discovering our own moral compass, and how/when to take calculated risks in sports and in life are critical skills, and we don't do a good enough job teaching this at schools.

Another underrated and forgotten "magic component" that comes from sports is the environment it creates for athletes to forecast and work toward something that doesn't exist yet. A big game, a scholarship, a tryout—it could be the only time in your life that, after doing all the forecasting and working toward the goal, you get to show off the work you've put in in front of thousands of people. What an awesome opportunity and good practice for looking ahead and working toward a goal. This is a skill the most successful humans practice and can do well.

Life is unpredictable and hard, and the goal shouldn't be to make life as easy as possible either. We just have to be ready and able to handle hardships, be tough, and learn how to make good decisions about the things we can control. This can come from playing sports. The following illustration shows some of these key zones of impact. Athletics provides the perfect opportunity to help athletes like you gain perspective through experiencing failure safely, gain tools to overcome adversity of any size, and learn the importance of character and integrity.

Impact-of-Choice Model—Youth Athletes

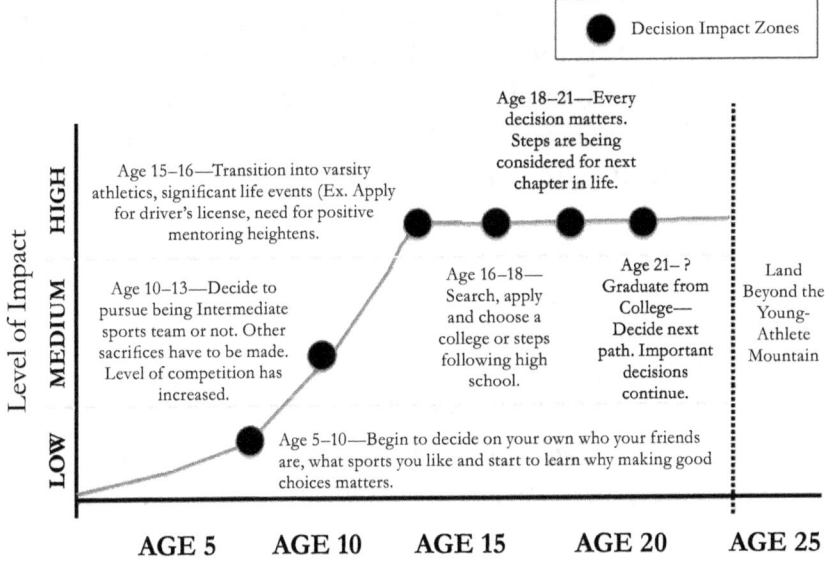

Age of Athlete

This model does not attempt to describe the path of "every" athlete but gives you an idea of some of the key zones of impact based on when important decisions must be made even early on. The other key to note here is the transitions that are happening between stages and why.

Tip: A common mistake I see being made by athletes is making decisions that don't align with what they think the outcome will be. Doing something because someone they knew did it that way or because they thought it was the only option or because of an adult's advice—it's critical that athletes are making decisions with the proper information and with the right motivations.

Who Is the Athlete Reading This Book?

The best athletes have confidence. Self-understanding can give you that confidence (even if it's knowing your weaknesses). It doesn't matter what others think you are or should be. It is up to you to decide. It will be your integrity, your character, and the principles that you live by that people will remember. This awareness will be critical in building the foundation to move forward. Bet on yourself, and others will too.

- ✓ *Where are you from?*
- ✓ *What do you value?*
- ✓ *What are your strengths/ weaknesses?*
- ✓ *Where is it that you want to go?*
- ✓ *What's preventing you from reaching your goals? Is it controllable?*
- ✓ *What is your "why"?*
- ✓ *What makes you unique?*
- ✓ *How do you want to be remembered?*

What Defines You?

It's fun to be a young athlete. You will have lots of opportunities to have fun and make memories with friends, but the fun times won't be what define you. Your legacy will be determined by what you do when times are tough, not easy, and what you do for others, not yourself. How you respond and learn from the times you don't get what you want will be far more important than the times you did. Let your time as an athlete reveal your character. Nobody is perfect, nor does anyone expect you to be; let who you are *now* define you, not who you were.

This book refers often to what we call "forming an alliance with adversity." You will begin to welcome the difficult times and appreciate them more than when things are easy. The more challenges there are, the better. Embrace the storm, see it as an opportunity, and accept the new challenges and the growth that will follow.

Why Have Our Paths crossed?

When I was a young athlete, there was nothing more important to me than being the best I possibly could, whatever that might be. I didn't want to be an athlete with regrets or miss having the information I needed during the time I really needed it. I experienced highs and lows just like every other athlete, and this pursuit would engulf the next twenty-plus years of my life. Being an athlete was the source of some of my best memories and skills that I acquired and still benefit from today, but it was also the source of large amounts of anxiety that took their toll on me physically and mentally. I committed to a two-decade approach of taking notes and reading everything I could as an athlete, kept learning as a coach of various levels and locations around the country, and have a perspective of the "land beyond" of being an athlete that I feel can help you avoid regrets and gain from what I collected along the way. I'm old enough to be a teacher and coach, but my days of being an athlete are recent enough that I haven't forgotten what it was like and know what you're feeling. I'm just another athlete and we might never meet, but you'll have a hard time finding anyone who cares more about giving back to this important part of life, *your* life, and there's a few reasons why.

In 2012, I was in my third year of coaching baseball at Hawaii Pacific University (HPU) and had recently started teaching at Punahou School. As the outdoor education teacher, it was part of my job to take each of the fourth grade classes from Oahu to Maui for a two-day/one-night trip. At approximately 4:45 a.m. on February 15th, I was on my way to my car to meet my students at the airport, and I discovered that someone had just broken into my '95 Nissan Pathfinder. I saw a guy down the street carrying a box. As he turned the corner, a baseball fell from his belongings. I knew then…it was my stuff. He really had only taken two items of value to me. My HPU baseball uniform and a pile of old, tattered notebooks. It was in these notebooks that I had been writing down notes, collecting quotes, and really every good piece of information I had been gathering for over two decades.

The short version: I chased him down, and I got my stuff back. Just as a gazelle has the lion to thank for its speed, I owe it to the car thief for the motivation to chase down what was important to me and share it before it was too late. If I had been there a few minutes later, if the baseball wouldn't have dropped, if I had not chased him down, much of what I spent years collecting and is now in this book would no longer exist.

My journey as a young athlete really began one summer in southern Minnesota when I met an athlete unlike any other. His name was Todd Mann. He wore #22. What happened next would change my life forever; it continues to impact me today, and it is the reason we now stand at the same crossroads together.

2
TM22 PART I

Every great athlete knows that nobody reaches the top of this mountain alone. If you want to make it to the top, it is critical that you are willing to ask for help along the way.

Coaches, parents, friends, teachers, a book—the source of support can come in many different forms. Some young athletes are fortunate to have many of these options available; some won't have any. Occasionally the support a young athlete receives will impact the rest of their life. It is this type of scenario that has brought you and me together.

While I was fortunate to have many people willing to share their time and energy with me, it was one athlete that had an impact on me that still remains. The following chapter will introduce you to an athlete named Todd Mann and explain why his story and what he represents can provide perspective, lessons, and maybe some inspiration to set yourself apart as an athlete and in life.

Why Should Todd's Story Matter to You?

You'll never meet Todd; he's not famous; he was a "normal" athlete that grew up in a small town, worked hard, wasn't perfect, and never claimed to be, but had a good heart. He achieved lots of athletic success, but his impact remains because of what he did for athletes just like you. The path you are on right now matters, just like Todd's, and your stories are now connected.

> "Now batting for the Waseca Braves...number twenty-two...Todd Mann."

Humidity and the smell of popcorn filled the air. It was a typical summer night at a Waseca Braves game at Tink Larson Field in Waseca, Minnesota, in the early '90s. The Braves were the local amateur baseball team comprised of a few boys from the high school team, collegiate players home for the summer, and a few guys just playing for the love of the game. Tink Larson Field was one of the best baseball atmospheres in the Midwest and the destination of many in town during the summer. On the microphone via the dugout was legendary coach Tink Larson himself.

During the 1950s, baseball was booming in Minnesota, and it's when Coach Larson's legend really began. He got his start as a head coach at the age of nineteen, coaching three teams, and experienced success right from the start. In 1967–1968, he made the move to Waseca and hasn't stopped coaching and taking care of the field, which is now named in his honor, and 2020 marked Coach Larson's 60th year mentoring young athletes. I was one of the fortunate athletes to learn far more than just baseball from Coach and was welcomed into a place that is now a second home to many.

Out of the dugout that night came Todd Mann, #22. His solid stature, grit, and determination to crush baseballs created a confident type of walking style only he could pull off. It was slow but purposeful. He was the catcher, leader of the team, and enemy to all opposing pitchers.

As he made his way to the batter's box, an eight-year-old kid looked on. It was me.

I had recently started my first job. The position: ball shagger. Baseballs were expensive, and the price of food in the concession stand was cheap. This combination of factors created a job description that would read as follows: "In the event there is a foul ball or home run, find the ball. Bring it back…no matter what."

This seemingly simple task becomes complicated when coupled with factors such as darkness, dogs, backyards with fences and clotheslines, disgruntled neighbors, curfew, and cars. It was these near insurmountable odds that also made it so much fun for an eight-year-old. The crack of the bat sending a ball into the night sky was like Thomas Jefferson sending Meriwether Lewis to venture across the United States in search of a water passage to the ocean. It was an adventure only a boy with extreme amounts of bravery could complete, or at least that's how I imagined it.

If you didn't lose a ball, you were paid $2.50 per game. This three-figure salary is a heavy incentive, but it wasn't what made me work so hard to do my job. I wanted the handshake and approval of Coach Larson. I wanted to play my role in helping a brotherhood of men that I watched so many summer nights growing up. I also wanted to make my parents proud and, at the end of the day, be proud of myself. Over twenty-five years later, these same motivating factors remain.

It was not only my first job but also my first opportunity to be a part of something bigger than myself. It was a chance to learn about a game as well as life. It was a chance to belong. I took great pride in never showing up empty-handed at the dugout and never left the park without spending all my earned wages at the concession stand. It was probably this combination that later led me to my first promotion from ball shagger to batboy.

I was young but can still remember how Coach Larson, his wife Sharon in the concession stand, Todd Mann, and all the other guys on that team treated me. Summer after summer, I would return to the ballpark to learn the game of baseball and so much more.

Tink Larson Field (Waseca, MN), early 1990s. Player on the left catching, wearing #22, Todd Mann. The batboy returning to the dugout was me.

It was these countless summer nights I spent perched on top of an electrical-transformer box that buzzed with electricity and mosquitoes, waiting in nervous anticipation for my next quest to find a baseball that I received my earliest lessons of how to be an athlete...and a man...and what that really meant. I watched every move the players made: how they played the game, how they treated each other, the timing and tone of what and when they shouted from the dugout, and how they went to battle for one another and experienced both success and failure together.

This is where it all began. This is when I knew I wanted to be not only an athlete but also an athlete who was remembered for all the right reasons. My quest to learn everything I could to reach my maximum potential as an athlete had begun.

Who is Todd Mann?

In 1964 Todd Mann was born in Bismarck, North Dakota. When he was six, he and his family moved to Waseca, Minnesota, a small, rural town surrounded by lakes, corn, and baseball fields. His childhood was like many in this part of the world, filled with hunting, fishing, working outside with his dad, and playing sports.

In high school, he spent much of his time with his sister Sherri, friend Mike, and his dad, Tink Larson. The Larsons were a baseball family. Today "Lars" is in a variety of baseball Hall of Fames and is one of Minnesota's most respected coaches. Todd became a son-like figure to Coach Larson, and they became great friends over the years. This would have a significant impact on Todd's life as a young athlete and, because of that, would go on to impact many others.

Todd played multiple sports, but baseball would be his future. After finishing his college baseball career at Southern Mississippi, he would eventually return home to Waseca. Summer after summer, he played with the Braves, crushing home runs and grilling steaks, and he really started to define himself off the field. His days of being a young athlete were over, but another important journey was just beginning.

For years Todd worked as the community education director, a position where he had an impact on players, coaches, and teachers throughout the town. Later on he became the high school athletic director, then the varsity baseball coach, and then a father to a great son. Throughout all of these positions, he served another important role: mentor.

For a few years before I was old enough to play on the Braves, Coach Larson allowed me to be part of the team. I ate sunflower seeds, ran the scoreboard, and if Todd ever got on base, I got to pinch run for him. I can still picture (and smell) that sweaty, pine-tar-covered, one-ear-flapped helmet he would hand me on his way back to the dugout. (I didn't break a lot of records as a collegiate athlete, but leading the conference in stolen bases and holding the program record for most career hits by pitches are accolades I credit to this early apprenticeship.)

Early one summer, the day I had trained for and dreamed of for years had finally arrived. It was my first real "moment of impact." I was in high school and was now able to get playing time with the Braves. We were in Chaska, Minnesota, and late in the game, Coach Larson told me I was going to get an at bat. It would be my first as a Brave. I was ready...well, almost ready.

I didn't have a bat. It seems odd to be a baseball player without a bat, but I was in high school and using wood bats was not common, and they were expensive, at least to me. At the other end of the dugout, sat #22. He was still playing. His walk to the plate had gotten even slower, but he could still play at a high level.

Todd called me down and pulled a bat from the bag beneath the bench. On the knob, he quickly wrote "A4" for my initial and number underneath his own T22. Not only was I about to have my first at bat, but it was also going to be with a bat owned by my hero. As I walked to the plate, I could already start to envision what was about to happen. It was just like a movie. A childhood hero gives the boy his first bat; he crushes a home run, the crowd goes wild, and an epic slow-motion high five and exchanged wink upon return to the dugout from the hero. I had so much confidence that even my walk to the plate resembled that of Todd Mann.

The first pitch I saw was right down the middle. I swung harder than I had ever swung before. I made contact—but not the good kind. As I held the handle of the bat, I watched the ball go in one direction and the barrel of the bat go in another. The ball blooped in behind the shortstop, and while it was a hit, it wasn't exactly how I had scripted it. I had broken my bat on the first pitch, on my first swing, and in my first at-bat, with a bat I had owned for less than twenty minutes. I still have the handle of that bat and wouldn't sell it for any amount of money.

Walking the Same Path...

No one had a bigger impact on my life as a young athlete than Todd Mann. We played for years together on the Braves; he became my high school baseball coach, opened the weight room for us before school, and gave me advice and his giant gray truck whenever I needed it. He hired me for my first coaching job in the Community Education Summer Baseball League. I worked for him in the athletic office while he was athletic director, and he got me the hardest job I ever had, working masonry with the Herschmans. All of these are experiences I still benefit from today.

One summer he built me a wooden locker to go with the others in the clubhouse located beneath the grandstand at Tink Larson Field. My journey at this ballpark had come full circle, from ball shagger to having my own locker in the clubhouse. It became both a family and a home.

After I graduated, I left Waseca and played college baseball at Augsburg College, and before I knew it, my days of being a young athlete had come to an end. I don't know that I was standing at the summit when this time came, but because of my experiences, hardships, and help along the way, I had the tools I would need for the land beyond the mountain.

The Day Everything Changed...

In the fall of 2009, I accepted a graduate assistant position with the Hawaii Pacific University baseball team. One day after practice, I received a call from one of Todd's best friends, Adam. We exchanged our usual few minutes of making fun of each other, and then Adam shared with me that Todd had recently gone to the doctor. Todd didn't like going to the doctor, so you knew he really wasn't feeling well if he had agreed to make the trip. There was nothing to worry about. Todd was a superhero, raising a great young boy of his own, still playing baseball for the Braves, and nothing could bring him down. He was invincible and the toughest guy I knew.

Not long after, Todd Mann would pass away from cancer that had spread throughout his body.

Near the end, the lady providing hospice care said he wouldn't last the day. Todd kept fighting. By his side were Coach Larson, his sister Sherri, and friends Adam and Mike. When Todd made his last gasp of air, Coach Larson looked at his watch; it was twenty-two minutes past midnight.

I don't recall the last time I saw Todd, what was said, or how I last said goodbye, but what I do know is that I never really told my boss, coach, mentor, hero, and now friend thank you.

From the time I was chasing down his home run balls as an eight-year-old to when I completed my collegiate baseball career, he treated me with the same amount of respect. He not only believed in who I was then but also in the person I wanted to become. It wouldn't be until years after he passed away that I realized why he had done so many things for me over the years, both on and off the field. He didn't do it because he wanted a thank-you. He did it because he cared about me as a human, not just an athlete. He did it because someone did the same for him, and he knew that someday I might have the opportunity to do the same for another young athlete.

Before you move on, take a minute to think about the people who have already helped you. Say thank you; show them you are grateful for how they've helped you on your journey by saying it, writing it, and through your actions. You never know when you might lose that chance. In the next chapter, we will attempt to define what we are chasing and why.

3

IN PURSUIT OF SUCCESS

Starting to gain an understanding of who we are was key; a critical next step is making the choice to pursue levels of success determined by you and aligning your actions with that pursuit.

If you don't have a clear vision of what being successful looks like to you, it's going to be difficult (if not impossible) to feel fulfilled as an athlete or in the life that follows. Like when a ship leaves a port and the captain has a destination to help navigate its course, athletes need to have a vision of what success is going to look like and *choose* to pursue that path.

Athletes that set goals are often more "successful" not because they always reach their goals but because those goals were a chosen direction to head in; it forced hard work, good habits, and consistent effort. (Tip: Don't worry as much about the specifics right now, and focus more on the process and environment you're creating around you. Your goals and how you define success are going to evolve, but right now is when you can build the foundation, vision, and habits that will allow you to build a life that allows you to be successful in a variety of ways.)

> "Excellence is never an accident. It is always the result of high intention, sincere effort, and intelligent execution; it represents the wise choice of many alternatives—choice, not chance, determines your destiny."
> —Aristotle

The two main goals of this chapter are: aligning actions and defining what success is and isn't. What you choose to do is up to you, but you need to be clear that a choice is being made. You're either choosing to just drift or choosing to work toward something.

> 1. **In pursuit** (working hard toward something). Specifics of what that something is not as important as you might think. Choosing to just drift along and just let the circumstances around you force you to conform isn't going to get you the things you really want as an athlete or in life.
>
> 2. **Of success** (a goal or direction you've determined as something that *you* want). If this thing is something you want to do and are passionate about, you'll work hard at it, so you'll be good at it. The key is being something you have defined for yourself, no one else.

What Is Success?

A trophy? Money? A feeling? There are a lot of definitions of success, and there should be. Our attempt to clarify this term is important not only to understand what it is but also what it is *not*. Learn this early, and commit to building your own definition throughout the rest of your life.

To help provide a foundation to build upon, here are a few other ways people, including athletes, have attempted to define success. In each type of definition, look for things you like but, maybe just as important, disagree with.

> **Success**—the accomplishment of an aim or a purpose.
> —(*Oxford Dictionary*)

This definition is about as basic as it gets, perhaps what makes it so strong. What it lacks, however, is any level of emphasis on the attempt or process. The journey it took to accomplish that goal has a significant impact on the weight of that success.

> **"(Natural Talent + Opportunity) Hard Work = Success"**
> —Michael Johnson (Olympic gold-medal sprinter)

Michael Johnson is one of the fastest people to ever walk (ok, maybe run) the planet. His hard work helped create the opportunity he had to run in the Olympics, but he definitely had some natural abilities most others don't. Maybe we can't control how much "natural talent" we have, but we can determine what we do with what we *do* have. In this equation, it just shows that, regardless of natural talent, if there is enough hard work, it can still equal success.

> **"The greatest enemy to tomorrow's success is sometimes today's success."**
> —John C. Maxwell, *Thinking for a Change*

One of the greatest motivators is the uncomfortable feeling that failure gives you. Therefore small amounts of success can sometimes be your worst enemy. If you want to get to the top, you're going to have to keep pushing yourself. Don't settle. Don't become complacent. We are in pursuit. Don't achieve small victories and be ok with that amount of success and stop. In this definition, the key to achieving success is to keep growing and improving.

> **"The most important thing is not to win, but to take part, just as the most important thing in life is not the triumph, but the attempt. The essential thing is not to have conquered, but to have fought well."**
> —(Olympic Creed 1894)

The value in this definition is the emphasis on the process and courage it takes to try and risk failure—not the outcome. You really have little control over how things will end, but you have all the control in the attempt and what you put in. This should give you comfort knowing that you don't have to worry about the uncontrollable factors and focus on doing your best. Maybe in the end, it's not the outcome but the effort that counts? Someday your success will be judged not on where you end up but on what you had to overcome to get where you are. Take pride in having to overcome more challenges than other athletes.

> **"Success is not a goal to reach or a finish line to cross. It is a system to improve, an endless process to refine."**
> —James Clear, *Atomic Habits: Tiny Changes, Remarkable Results*

This definition is from James Clear's book *Atomic Habits: Tiny Changes, Remarkable Results*, a book I highly recommend. There's so much we can't control, and yet it's common for us to spend the most time on those very things. If we can create the right environment with the right systems, composed of the right components, we'll have a better chance of achieving the results that we want. Clear shares that "we don't rise to the level of our goals but fall to the level of our systems." This is critical to remember, and focusing on the process rather than just results is something elite athletes talk about often. Specific goals at times can even be restrictive and confining; it's common that, if you focus on the process, you'll achieve peripheral goals that turn out to be even better than the ones you had hoped for.

If we're products of our decisions, our habits, and our routines, then the focus should be placed here. I don't think stating or writing goals should be eliminated, but it needs to be understood that the actions we take every day are what are getting us closer or further away from our goals. If you can design and operate in an environment that encourages steps in the right direction, that's the system you want and could result in reaching goals you didn't even think possible.

Tip: A mistake I see athletes make is saying how important chasing excellence is, but the habits don't match the goals. You can't expect extraordinary results from ordinary habits and behaviors. "I went to practice just like everyone else." That's the problem; what else did you do?

You must create the environment, set up the routines you need to pull the best out of you, and stick to them. Find a routine that works; be consistent. You get what you put in.

What Does This Pursuit Look Like?

The line between where you are now and what you're trying to get isn't a straight, direct line. Some of the turns, corrections, and maneuvers required are out of your control—that's life. What is in your control is learning to catch yourself and get back on track. Those that excel can identify this early, make changes efficiently, and do whatever it takes to keep moving forward.

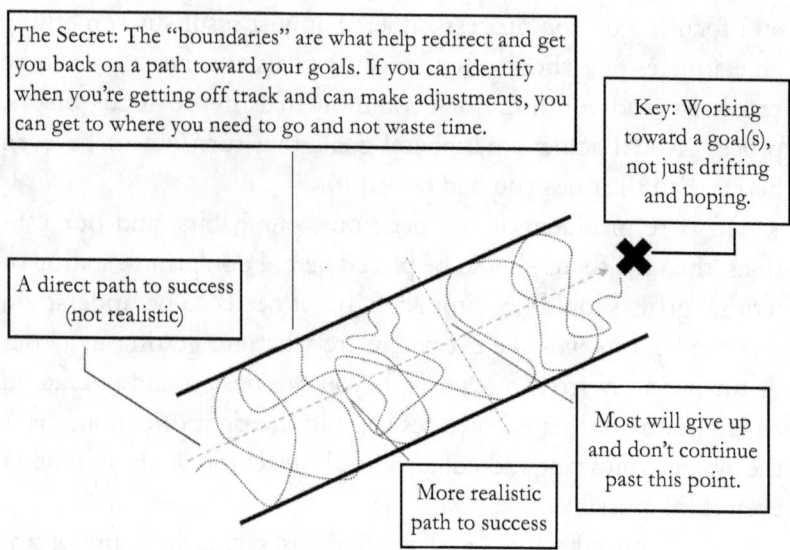

The Secret: The "boundaries" are what help redirect and get you back on a path toward your goals. If you can identify when you're getting off track and can make adjustments, you can get to where you need to go and not waste time.

Key: Working toward a goal(s), not just drifting and hoping.

A direct path to success (not realistic)

Most will give up and don't continue past this point.

More realistic path to success

Tip: Catch yourself if you feel like you're getting off track, and your path will be more direct, efficient, and possible. Others will try to determine what success is or isn't for you, but remember—it's not up to them. Ask for help but trust your instincts. It's common for elite athletes to have a symbol, a phrase, or an object acting as a reminder that gets them back on track and on course for their goals. Sometimes you have to pause, even circle back, to move forward again.

How to Build Your *Own* Vision and Strategy for Success

Building your own definition of success and vision can last a lifetime. Knowing yourself, keeping an open mind, and being flexible will be key. (It is a common mistake early on to define what you're chasing by a dollar amount, an object, or a statistic. It is also important to remember that while it is helpful to understand how others define their pursuit, it is different for everyone, and you need to be able to understand the whole path traveled. You are the only one who knows that path and what you've gone through. Wealth, fame, and trophies often mask the true successes made and can be dangerous if those few descriptors are the only options for success.)

1. Find a Path(s) Toward Success that Fits *You*

> "Nothing great was ever accomplished without inspiration."
> —Earl Nightingale, *The Strangest Secret*

Your definition will and should look different from those around you. It's ok to want to make your family proud, but in the end, you are the only judge of whether you are successful, and you should continue this pursuit throughout your entire life in every endeavor. Focus on your day-to-day actions, your routines, and your habits, and continuously ask yourself if those choices are moving you closer to or further from your goals.

Most people will wander through life, waiting to see what life chooses for them. Pick a direction. Identify the obstacles. Use your habits to move you toward the goal. Even if your destination changes, you are moving forward and doing what you can to dictate your own destiny. Someone, someday, is going to be impacted by the choices you're making now. This includes you.

Why You Need to Be You
If you're not you, now, no one will ever be. The amount of pressure you feel to conform is going to increase throughout life, especially as you near various levels of success that others haven't been able to reach themselves. Find your niche, don't let others decide who you really are, and remember that no one's calling is more important than another's. You may never know the impact that "being you" will have on another person, this planet, and the future. Think about all those who came before you in order for you to be able to be you. If you try to be something or someone else, even if you "succeed," you will regret it and feel like you gave up on the person you were meant to be.

Tip: It's common for athletes to feel like their parents have a pretty clear vision of what success should look like for them, but what happens if you don't agree or are thinking, "I'm fourteen years old; how would I know that right now"? Ultimately your parents should want you to be happy and pursue something you're passionate about. For now, do things that open doors. Work hard. Be a good person. Apply the skills and lessons shared in this book and work toward a goal.

2. Dream Big and Have the Courage to Take Steps toward That Vision

It's important to dream big, but it can also be the easy part. It's identifying the steps and then actually taking them that takes courage to make that vision a reality. There are going to be times where you may have to put yourself out there and take some chances. They say that the reason why obstacles and "brick walls" preventing you from getting to where you want to go exist is to keep out the people that don't want it bad enough. If it were easy, everyone would do it. If you really want something, you can overcome it. It may require you to do more than what the others around you are doing, but if you want more than what others have, that's the price you'll pay.

Tip: Don't sell yourself short. Can you think of something you can be a part of that you can't accomplish in your lifetime? A common mistake is not dreaming at all or only dreaming big. Dream of things you never thought possible, and then look at the steps it's going to take to get there. Don't limit yourself, and don't put unnecessary roadblocks in your own way.

3. Adapt Your Definition of Success over Time, but Don't Settle

Over time, things change. People change. Sports change. Our priorities will change. This is natural. But the importance of trying to do the right thing, being accountable for yourself, and wanting to exceed expectations and follow your passions are things that should never change.

The planet has shown us throughout history that those who are willing and able to adapt are the ones who are the most successful. Once you are aware of how things are changing, you have to be willing to try new things, think differently than you once did, and take action accordingly. These times to adapt may take place in the weight room or at practice, but also with your family, friends, and how you see the world around you. Things are going to change; you might as well embrace it and use it as yet another way to set yourself apart. Be careful, however, not to settle for something that falls below what you believe you're capable of doing. The world is full of traps that will hope you'll fall in line and be like everyone else, buy things, follow the norm, and help others reach their own dreams. Have the courage to take steps toward what you believe in.

Tip: Your willingness to chase this goal and overcome obstacles is an important success alone. Do what makes you proud when you look in the mirror, don't worry about how others choose to define success for themselves, and know that whatever happens, it is your journey that will one day define you, and this should feel good.

How Does the Definition of Success for TM22 Athletes Differ from Other Athletes?

Some athletes compete because they want to be the best, reach their maximum potential, chase scholarships and NIL deals, and make themselves and their families proud. Some athletes put a high value on principles, use sports to show and grow their character, and want to leave behind a legacy of integrity. Some athletes want both, as athletes and in life. Don't choose between one or the other. Be both. (Having fun and being with your friends can be in both scenarios, but your sacrifices and time spent in sports should be more than that.) The term TM22 athlete is being used here to symbolize an approach for athletes that are on a pursuit to reach their maximum potential and an athlete of character.

(Note: We have been using the journey up a mountain as a metaphor, but there can be danger in this. At the top of a mountain, there is a summit, a destination, and an ending point. Or at least it seems this way. The journey gives a chance to gain perspective of what lies ahead and the tools and experiences needed to get there. However, the summit is only a place to pause along your quest. The TM22 athlete will use this perspective to look back, appreciate the obstacles they have overcome, and then look to the horizon in search of yet another mountain to climb. The journey of every athlete is different, but elite athletes have the courage to "choose" excellence.

Where your life leads and where you end up is the outcome of millions of interconnected choices: Choice to get better. Choice to work hard. Choice to sacrifice. Choice to care. Not making a choice is a choice.)

TM22 Philosophy: Your trajectory is created by choice, not chance. If you don't like where you're heading or want something more, make the choice to change it. You are responsible for determining who you want to be and must take ownership of the path to get there.

TM22 Core Beliefs:

1. TM22 athletes value integrity. They aren't choosing between reaching their maximum potential as athletes and leaving behind a legacy they're proud of—they are in pursuit of both.
2. TM22 athletes refuse to be ordinary. Hard work, sacrifices, and accountability are important to these athletes, and they're willing to show the sustained discipline needed to set themselves apart.
3. TM22 athletes belong to an alliance. These athletes care about more than just themselves and, when able, will seek ways to give back and make the path better for future athletes.

The young-athlete journey contains large amounts of rapid change. These core beliefs are important to remember and will keep us on course. The best athletes also know that we will ultimately be defined by more than just stats, trophies, and wins. Are those goals? Sure. But our definition of success doesn't stop there.

Important: TM22 athletes aren't perfect nor claim to be better than others but are always trying to improve, are humble, and *are committed to a sustained effort and pattern of actions over time.* It's never too late to start and/or make a change, and you don't need anyone's permission. You can be both humble and hungry, you can be a competitor but not be known for barking at the refs every possession or using it as an excuse; and you can take care of yourself and be a good teammate.

The following illustration shows the journey of five athletes, one of whom is a TM22 athlete. Follow along to see the patterns most athletes follow and the reasons why TM22 athletes will reach success on this mountain and many more.

The Journey of Five Athletes

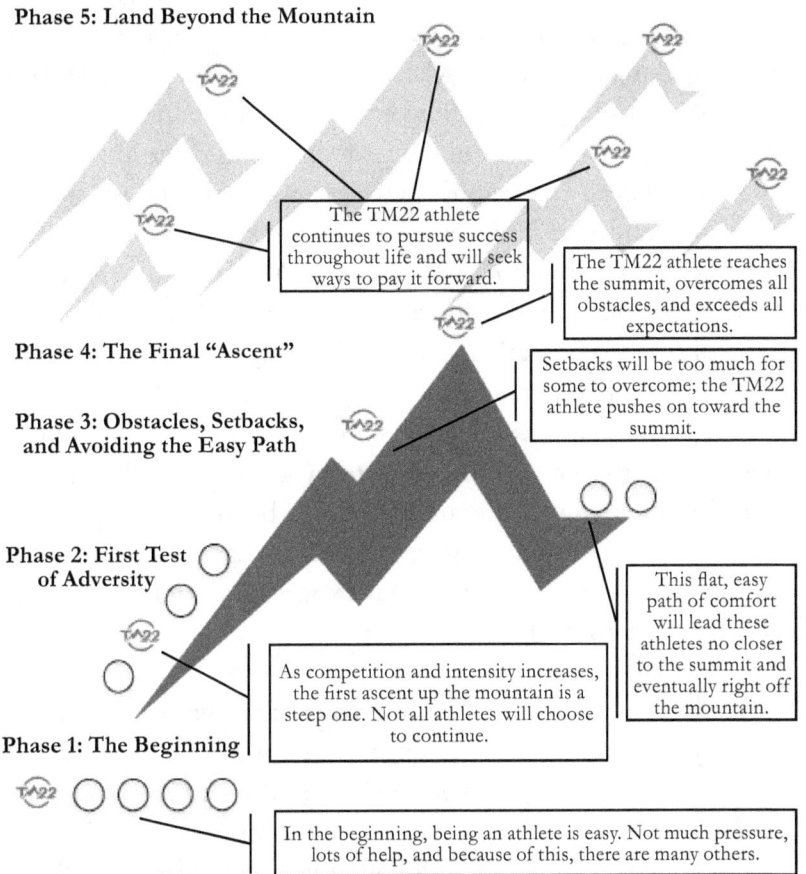

Note: Not every little thing you do deserves praise. Showing up on time, working hard, and having a good attitude are expected and shouldn't have to be rewarded. *It's just what you do.*

A key point this illustration is trying to make is that a lot of athletes will start this journey, but when adversity emerges, it's where the journey ends. Use adversity to your advantage.

What happens in the future is the product of the decisions you're making today. If you want success later in life, the game plan to follow is like the one used to get on track for pursuing a championship in a season later in the year. Success is determined in the months between and leading up to seasons, not by the athlete who tried the hardest during that game or week. What is it that you want ten years from now, which you can't have quite yet, but the time between now and then will determine whether you get it? It's kind of scary to think that if you really, really want it, you can have it if you're willing to put in the work and make sacrifices.

The next chapter will share some of the research being done and advice from other young athletes who have come before you. This information will help us continue to build perspective, avoid common mistakes and regrets, and ensure that we are navigating in a direction that aligns with our expectations and building the habits that support that quest.

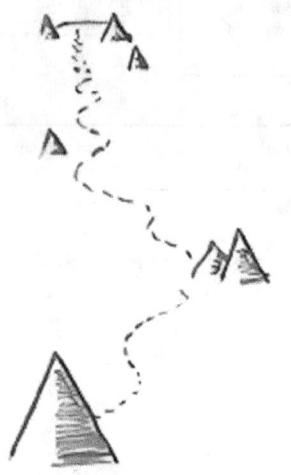

> **"To live your life in your own way, to reach for the goals you have set for yourself, to be the you that you want to be—that is success."**
> —Terry Orlick, *In Pursuit of Excellence: How to Win in Sport and Life Through Mental Training*

4

TRACKING FORMER ATHLETES—RESEARCH, DATA, AND ADVICE

The art of tracking was a critical skill for early humans; it's also important for young athletes.

Perhaps the oldest science, tracking can be defined as "examining detectable evidence of something that has passed." This skill offers us directions to follow or avoid. The key will be to know which is which and remember that you, too, are being followed. Success as an athlete (and beyond) is an elusive, wild animal. The more knowledge we have about what we're chasing and the environment it is in, the better our chances of finding it. The best trackers weren't necessarily the strongest or fastest, but the most knowledgeable, patient, and perseverant. The art of tracking may hold secrets to how we are wired, what gives us fulfillment, and the skills needed to be successful in our pursuit of excellence as athletes and beyond.

One of the original drivers of this book was the desire to learn from those who went through some of the same things I did. What can I learn from others that will help me reach my maximum potential? How do I make the most of my time as a young athlete? Was I making the same mistakes other young athletes have made? How do I avoid having regrets? Am I alone?

Who Cares What Other Athletes Think and What They Went Through?

During the transition from being a young athlete to coach to teacher, I continued to listen to athletes begin sentences that started with: "I could have reached my maximum potential if only I would have known..." "If I could go back and do it all over again, I would definitely..." "I would have given anything to know..." "My biggest regret is definitely..."

What would happen if athletes knew these things while they were still playing and before it was too late? Do current athletes know that former athletes want to and are willing to help them on their quest? What if there was a way for former young athletes to share these things with future young athletes? Would it make a difference? This chapter attempts to help us find out.

Former Young Athletes Heading Toward the Summit

Master trackers use what they call an "anthropomorphic way of thinking," which basically means trying to put yourself in the shoes of whatever it is that you're chasing so you better understand it, where it's going, etc. Who do you know who is successful? Is there someone that you know who has what you want? What steps do you think they had to take for them to get there?

Over time the answer to those questions will change. Your definition of success can and should adapt, which means the examples of success you see will change as well. This is normal. Our admiration for what others have had to overcome should grow, and acknowledging their final destination should fade.

If we are going to track those who came before us, we want to make sure we are following the right tracks. This doesn't necessarily mean we can't learn from those who made lots of mistakes, but following those who scattered their paths with regrets is dangerous and not where we want to go. There aren't shortcuts, <u>but there are opportunities to streamline your pursuit of your goals and make more of your short window to be an athlete count by taking the right paths.</u>

Tracking Athletic Excellence

The best trackers can not only tell what kind of tracks were left behind and the direction they are going but also what that thing was doing, how it was feeling, and what it was going to do next. That's what you need to become. The following illustration looks at a series of tracks left by those on very different paths. Whether you realize it or not, you're following one or the other.

Animal 1: Mediocrity
(Mediocre: "Just being average or ordinary")

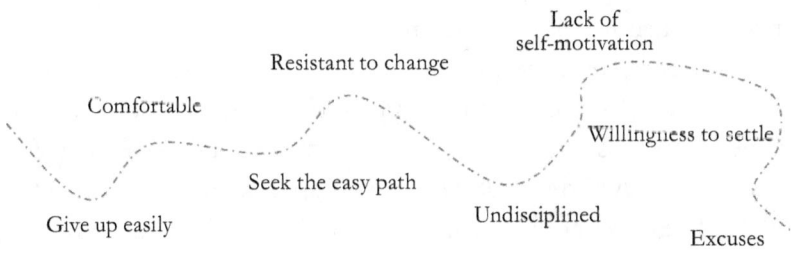

Animal 2: Excellence
(Excellence: "Achieving levels of success, maximum potential, set apart from other athletes")

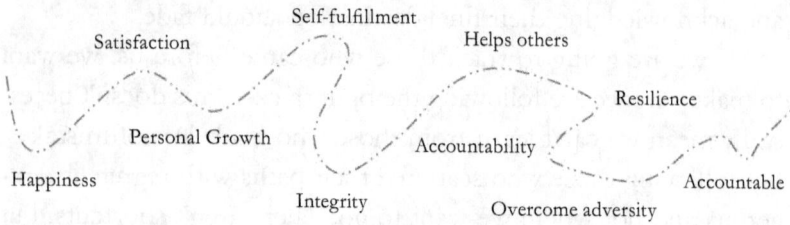

What tracks are you following right now? What do the tracks that you're leaving behind say?

When I was in first grade, there was a fourth grader at my school named Barry. He was fast; he could kick the kickball onto the roof of the school; even his name was cool. Someday I wanted to be just like him. I watched him on the playground, how he acted around his friends, and especially how he played sports. Even as a seven-year-old, I knew that, if I wanted to be a fourth-grade stud, it wouldn't be a bad idea to do the things he was doing. He had what I wanted. Those were the tracks I was going to follow for as long as I could. One day, on the way home from school, I stopped to look down at my untied shoe. I felt a hand on my shoulder; it was Barry. He looked at me and said, "Hey, keep your head up." I didn't tell him I was just looking down because my shoe was untied; I just smiled and nodded my head.

Think of someone who has what you want. What did they do to get there? Modeling your actions after someone who has the type of success that you want is a great idea. Be wise about following blindly though; others are equipped with a different set of skills. I never was able to kick a ball on the roof like Barry did, but

I do think I worked harder and became a better athlete because I tried to do what I could to get there. Remember you control the process, not the outcome.

The Phases of Tracking Success

There is a lot we can learn from animals. It's common for animals when they hunt or even travel from one spot to the next; it begins by following the beaten path made by what they're chasing. It's efficient, saves energy, and gives them the exact direction they need to go. There's no reason to not use what other animals have learned to their advantage, but as they approach what they're chasing, they will diverge from the beaten path, probe for opportunities, and, when their moment arrives, have the courage it takes to attack. The best athletes follow this same model. What we're chasing might change, but the need to adapt and blaze our own trails sometimes will not.

Phase 2
In this phase, many will quit, get lost, or lose motivation. The goal is in sight; this is your opportunity to diverge, blaze your own trail, and get ready to attack your moment.
Tip: Just doing what everyone else is doing isn't going to be enough.

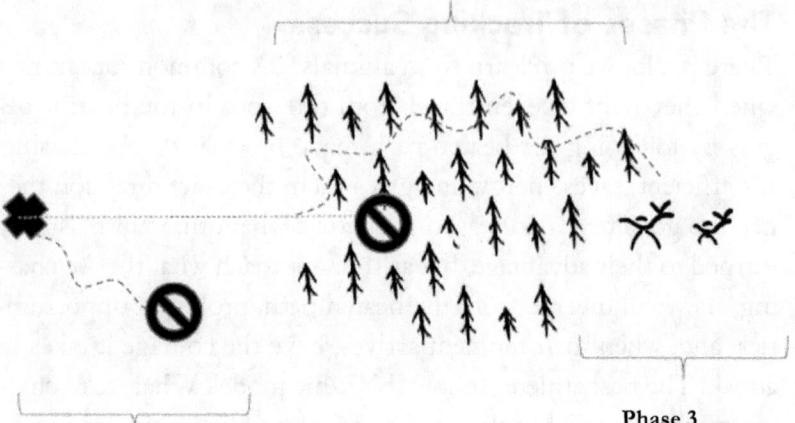

Phase 1
Follow the beaten path in the beginning, take advantage of learning from those before you, avoid common mistakes, and apply the lessons they already uncovered for you.

Phase 3
You've put in the work. Time to finish. It's up to you to do the work.

(Keys to the illustration above: If you are "hunting" success, you must possess the skills to track it, the sustained discipline to keep going when a new trail is needed and have the courage to attack when you find it.)

Phase 1: Follow the Tracks: Advice from Those Who Care

You need to learn to identify people who genuinely care about what happens to you beyond sports or a season. These are the people who aren't in it for personal gain, to live vicariously through you, or for their own sense of pride. They want what is best for you. If you have people like this in your life, you are fortunate. The following section contains advice from people who genuinely want to see you succeed and care about your life as an athlete and what comes after.

The sample of data I include here was collected through ongoing informal conversations, formal surveys, and data requests from former athletes and coaches of various sports, levels, abilities, and purposes. It is not listed in order of importance or categorized by how common it is. It is also not designed for you to just accept these things and make them your own. Some may apply, but some may not. Look for patterns and similarities and use them to build your own perspective.

Below are examples of common questions that I use:

> "What does today's young athlete need to know?"
> "What are the biggest challenges facing young athletes today?"
> "As a young athlete, is there any one thing you wish you would have known early on?"
> "What do young athletes need to know about the journey after their athletic days are over?"
> "If you could do it all over again, would you do anything differently? If so, what?"

Sample of Responses

Note: This sample does not claim to include every perspective but does offer an idea of what kind of information was gathered in hopes we can identify themes. Find ways to continue to collect your own data and perspective will grow.

"What does today's young athlete need to know?"

> - *Enjoy the process. Athletics can provide a range of experiences and emotions like no other activity, and as a result, the learning is limitless. Enjoy the hard work, the camaraderie, the successes and the "failures," and the lessons of working together to achieve a common goal.*
> - *Play a sport because you enjoy it. Don't play for someone else. Play with passion, energy, and love for what you're doing.*
> - *It's ok to fail. It's how you respond to that failure that is important.*
> - *Be present. When a coach is talking, make eye contact. How you carry yourself matters.*
> - *Don't worry about statistics; it's your character that will be remembered.*
> - *Your true character and reflection of how you were raised show in how you act in the locker room, classroom, and home, not just at practice. Be grateful. Be respectful.*
> - *The lessons learned on the field in competition, in preparation, and the brotherhood gained along the way have been a guiding force throughout my life.*
> - *Have fun and enjoy the experience, both in adversity and in glory, because there's always something to learn that helps you become a better person.*
> - *Remember to give your body proper amounts of rest, take breaks, and mix up use of muscles to prevent overuse injuries.*
> - *Take advantage of the life lessons that sports teach. Teamwork, working hard at practice, winning with dignity, losing with grace, developing skills that are important to fulfill the job expectations, and having fun.*

> *Fuel your body with the proper nutrition so you're able to do this.*
> *Work hard—sometimes things just don't work out, but if you worked as hard as you could, you will have no regrets.*
> *If you have a coach (or parent) that demands discipline and respect and isn't just trying to be your friend, you will one day be very grateful for this. Say thank you.*

"What are the biggest challenges facing young athletes today?"

> *Some don't have enough opportunities, some have too many, and most aren't given good advice on what is the right amount for them.*
> *Early specialization can lead to injuries, burnout, and a lack of opportunity to gain skills and perspectives from playing different sports and learning from different types of coaches.*
> *External pressure from parents, society, traveling teams, and oversaturation of a single sport or activity seem to correlate to decreased passion for their sport, repetitive motion injuries, and burnout.*
> *Balancing school, social life, and health, there's a lack of teaching kids how to find this balance. Health and school shouldn't suffer because of being a young athlete.*
> *Social media/instant communication: It's easy to get distracted with "noise" about who said this and this person is doing that...kids need to focus on themselves and just try to get better each day.*
> *A rising number of coaches discourage playing other sports to benefit their own team, and this is not in the best interest of the athlete.*
> *There are high (and often unrealistic) expectations from parents at an early age.*
> *With more and more options to get additional lessons, showcases, and all-star teams, it is expensive and gives the impression that one must do all just to keep up.*

- *Entitlement attitude: Athletes are being told they are entitled to certain things and have a difficult time dealing with failure or being told they have to earn things. A lot of this stems from parent perception, and kids are being robbed of learning these lessons.*
- *Allowing athletes to experience failure and the "tough times" to can gain perseverance, develop coping skills to overcome anxiety, and deal with pressure.*
- *Competition is good, but at the right times and amounts; we've lost sight of that balance.*

"As a young athlete, is there any one thing you wish you would have known early on?"

- *You are not alone. The position you are in and the challenges you face are those of many.*
- *Training techniques, the importance of proper nutrition, and strength and conditioning.*
- *Don't compare yourself to others. Be yourself. And be proud of being you.*
- *Play multiple sports and enjoy them all. It's ok not to be the best in every sport; it will provide you with a valuable perspective and allow for growth in the others.*
- *It's ok to fail. I wish I would have responded differently and not been so hard on myself.*
- *My success/failure does not define me.*
- *It's ok to make mistakes. It was hard to play at times because the pressure to be the best was always there. It was hard.*
- *Helping and building up others will not only help you grow as an athlete, but it will also help you forge positive relationships that will last a lifetime.*
- *How important the mental side of athletics is. It is important to get*

> used to the feelings of being anxious and nervous and learn how to deal with it and be comfortable.
> What you do in school and what grades you get matter. For example, when college coaches are looking at you, skill is part of it, but how you do in school can make or break a college's ability to bring you in. Don't limit your options by not trying in school.
> If it's important to you, you can make time. Think outside the box. Set yourself apart.

"What do young athletes need to know about the journey after their athletic days are over?"

> *Athletics is something that can stay with you your whole life. The lessons you learned on and off the field can stay with you and help you for your entire life. Time management, drive, perseverance, hard work, cooperation/collaboration, and of course camaraderie are pieces of your athletic career that will always be with you to guide and help you.*
> *Just because your playing days are over doesn't mean your athletic days are over. Stay active, stay involved, stay in shape, and develop a healthy lifestyle.*
> *Find a passion and give back. Help fellow travelers along their journey. Journey together, and enjoy it!*
> *Continue to work hard to build relationships on whatever team or group you are a part of. Enjoy every moment you have with them, and celebrate the successes along the way with humility.*
> *You have a responsibility to "pay it forward." Somewhere along your journey, you had someone who made a difference for you, and you should do the same for another. The world would be a better place if we all did that.*
> *Remember who you played for and who you went to battle with. Use*

> *the same skills you learned playing sports in your everyday life; you'll be amazed at how similar sports and life are.*
> *A lot of people made sacrifices for you; say thank you, be respectful, and be appreciative of the impact they had on your life.*
> *You should take the values and friendships you developed and use them to help you lead a good, balanced life.*
> *Be proud of what you have accomplished. Appreciate the little things. Do whatever you can to give others those same opportunities and show them you care.*
> *It's hard to be a coach or a parent; try to understand their perspective and challenges.*
> *You will learn some of the most important lessons in life by playing sports, make sure you acquire those skills, and regardless of what happens, you will leave without regrets.*
> *No one really will care about the stats and trophies, but they will remember how you played.*

"If you could do it all over again, would you do anything differently? If so, what?"

> *I would have taken proper nutrition and rest more seriously. Doing this can have a huge impact on your body, especially during a time of growth and maturation.*
> *I once chose not to attend a camp because I was afraid I wasn't good enough. I wish I would have gone and not worried about things I couldn't control and taken more chances.*
> *I wish I would have enjoyed the journey more; at times I took it too seriously.*
> *Better offseason training and rest to avoid injury.*
> *The timing of when and how to work hard. Championships aren't*

> *won during the season; they are won by those willing to do the extra work in the offseason.*
> *I would have worried less about statistics.*
> *Focus on enjoying it more; the time spent playing sports goes by quickly!*
> *I was too concerned about winning and paired winning with success. The result was pressing too much and not appreciating the process as much as I should have.*
> *The one thing I would do differently would be to not put so much pressure on myself. I would have concentrated more on being a student first, then an athlete.*
> *I would have said thank you more and showed that I was appreciative by making better choices off the field.*
> *I let a bad coach impact my potential as an athlete by using it as an excuse. I should have looked for things I could have learned and succeeded in spite of them.*
> *I took for granted putting on a uniform and what it meant to represent my school, my teammates, and my family.*
> *I would have taken more chances and more risks. I cared so much that I was tentative about making mistakes.*
> *I know I was a better teammate when things were going well for me. I now understand the importance of doing my job even when times are tough, and that shows true character.*

Can you identify any trends within the sample of advice given? Can you relate to any of these? If you were asked these same questions, what would you say? Again, apply this advice to your own perspective, and continue to listen. And remember, I'm just one former athlete asking other athletes, coaches, and parents that I know; ask the people around you these questions.

What Does the Research Say and Why Does It Matter?

Ultimately, taking the word of those who shared this journey should be enough, regardless of what the research says. However, it is reassuring to know that there is a lot of substantive, research-based data that supports what we believe. You can do more research but for the purpose of this book and time here's a quick example that should make you feel good about your path.

In an article from the *Journal of Leadership and Organizational Studies* entitled "Sports at Work: Anticipated and Persistent Correlates of Participation of High School Athletics," two studies examined how participation in competitive youth sports was correlated with success beyond the days of being a young athlete. The studies were looking specifically at whether being a young athlete made you a better employee and used criteria involving leadership, self-confidence, self-respect, time management, and willingness to volunteer and donate to charity. If you think about the principles passed on to young athletes at an early age, this shouldn't be much of a surprise. What's encouraging is that data shows success both short- and long-term, and there is tangible evidence that shows the worth of all the sacrifices made early on.

> "Athletes tend to be successful outside of sports because they learn that life doesn't just hand us everything, that some people excel more than others, and that such excellence comes from preparation and work."
> —Dan Millman, *Body Mind Mastery: Creating Success in Sports and Life*

Phase 2: Identify the Time to Diverge and Blaze Your Own Trail

Research and detectable evidence left by former athletes will only last so long. The groomed trail will eventually end. There will come a point where we can no longer rely on data and following the footsteps of others. You now must decide if you are willing to do what it takes. This can be a challenging time for athletes because there's no longer a coach or parent standing behind them telling them exactly what to do and what to eat—it has to be self-driven. You may still be doing the same practices and playing on the same summer teams as other athletes in your area, but the time has come that you have to do more. Just doing what everyone else is doing is no longer enough, not if you want to set yourself apart and find the level of success you're looking for. Ask yourself, *Why would I do what everyone else is doing if I wanted a different outcome than them?*

Regardless of what happens in your quest as a young athlete, remember the power of "doing the extra." Pay attention; be observant; even when you can no longer see tracks in front of you to simply follow, you'll know enough about what you're chasing, the speed you need to go, and the direction you need to be heading in so you can't miss it.

Phase 3: Show the Courage to Take a Chance

It's easy to follow the paths of others or just do what your mom and dad tell you to do, but eventually it has to come from you, and only you, and can require some risk and making decisions that have sacrifices. It could impact your social life or the amount of time you spend on social media, but choosing to act can also impact where your journey as an athlete goes next.

Sometimes these moments are predictable—maybe it's the championship game, the last possession in the fourth quarter, a showcase—but they don't all happen on a court or field. The best athletes will tell you that where they set themselves apart was the work they put in during the time between seasons when no one was looking. A mistake I see athletes make is wondering why they're not seeing results and achieving anything more than those around them, and it doesn't seem fair because they're going to practice and do the same amount of reps and work as everyone else. If you want more, you have to be willing to do more, and that can take courage.

Tip: Find your niche, use the things that make you unique to set you apart, and worry less about the specifics and more about pushing yourself to keep improving every day. Even as you and your goals change, you will have created the environment and habits to create good results.

The next chapter provides some of the most important skills, lessons, and athlete truths to help you in your pursuit toward whatever types of levels of success you're after.

> **"If you want something you've never had, you are going to have to do something you've never done."**
> —Thomas Jefferson

5

THE ATHLETE OUTPOST— KEY SKILLS AND LESSONS CRITICAL TO YOUR QUEST

Quests take the traveler a long way from where they began, internally and externally. An outpost is a place you would stop at along the way to make sure you were equipped for the journey ahead.

For decades I have sought ways to equip first myself and other athletes like you with the skills they will need to continue and experience success in whichever path they may choose. The obstacles have changed, the athletes have changed, and the buzzwords have changed, but there are some valuable key skills that will always be important to athletes. These are the skills provided here and are immune to rapidly changing conditions.

Hundreds of tips, skills, and lessons have made their way to this outpost over the years, but the ones provided to you in this chapter have stood the test of time. Some may seem obvious, and some may be something you are already good at. There also will be some that challenge you and will cause you to think in a way you never have before. This is good. It is up to you to decide how, if, and when you should use them. It's another choice you'll have to make as an athlete. All the lessons and tips included are within your control. They don't depend on genetics, talent, or size. They depend on how badly you want them and what legacy you truly want to leave behind.

Why a List of 22?

Just as there is danger in using climbing a mountain as a metaphor for our story, compiling a list can make it appear as if these skills are more important than others. This isn't true here. Consider it a collection for you to add to your quiver and add as you see fit.

(Note: Numerology is the study of numbers and looks at how they may impact our lives. You can do more research and choose to believe in this or not, but you should know that some believe that 22 is the most powerful number. Athletes live in a world surrounded by numbers. It's also associated with being able to manifest your dreams into reality. It could all be a coincidence, or it could be a reminder to stay focused and trust in the process of reaching your goals.)

TM22: Key Skills and Lessons Critical to Your Quest

The following section contains skills, advice, and lessons, along with a brief explanation of each.

The best way to use this part of the book is to come back to it from time to time, write in it, discuss it with others, and use it to start making your own list. You may notice that one thing all of these lessons have in common is that they require you to take action. Don't wait; figure out a way to implement them in your life right away, and do it with some urgency.

1. Make a Plan: The Power of Forecasting
You don't need me to tell you that, as an athlete, things don't always go as planned. And you've probably been told you need a plan; you need to set goals, you need to do the work required to reach those goals, but elite athletes can adjust and take planning a level above. Organizing and acting on the things you can see and you know you need to do is important, but the magic comes from *leveraging the adjustments you can make along the way before others*. You need to make a plan, not a wish, and be ready and willing to adapt that plan. Finding your own motivation to train for an opportunity that can't be seen or doesn't exist yet is something elite athletes do.

Along your quest, there will be things that you can control and predict, but also many factors that you cannot. If you want to set yourself apart, be ready for adversity and avoid missing opportunities; you need to see what's approaching on the horizon before others. Having a plan is a good start, but if you want to be great, you need to be ready to know when that plan needs to change.

The Power of Forecasting
The best athletes and coaches make plans that help identify what may lie ahead and be prepared for it. The ability to "forecast" is a level above. If you're constantly just reacting, waiting for life to happen to you, or fixing mistakes from the last game, you'll always be behind. Ask yourself things like, "What is happening six months from now that I could be preparing for? Challenges? Opportunities?

What aren't other people thinking of?" The longer you wait, the less chance you will have to take advantage of an opportunity, and the more people you will have to battle with. If you get into the habit of continued forecasting, you can stay ahead of the pack. Others will wonder how you are always ready, prepared, and find yourself in the right situations—it's because you've been forecasting. Your goals and principles can remain; the plan on how you get there should continue to adapt. It can be easy to set goals and make a long-term plan, but most people aren't willing to do what it takes each day to get there. If you can accomplish your small plans, it will lead to big results. The specifics will work themselves out as you get closer, you just have to make sure you're in range.

> **"All successful coaches and players have at least one thing in common: a strong game plan."**
> —Lou Holtz

Lou Holtz is a legendary football coach and great ally of young athletes. He knows that having a strong game plan includes not only a good plan A but also having a plan when things change.

If things don't go as planned and you need to change, that's ok; at least you know that things didn't go as planned and need to recalibrate. If you don't have a plan, you will never know, and will just be wandering aimlessly, hoping that something good will happen. Make a plan and establish a routine, but be willing and able to adapt, keep forecasting, and keep your focus on the process.

2. Learn to Finish the Things That Matter
Don't be an "almost athlete"—someone who starts things but doesn't finish, almost does the right thing, is almost a good

teammate. See it through. Starting something is easy; a lot of people do that; finishing it isn't; that's why so few are able to do it. Sometimes people stop because of the risk and sacrifice, and sometimes people stop because the feeling right before it feels good enough not to have to finish.

A common difference between those that are successful and those that aren't—they finished whatever it was that they started. The world is full of people who will just do the bare minimum and then complain about not getting more or offer a solution. It doesn't mean they didn't fail; failing is a valuable lesson you can only gain by actually finishing.

Tip: It's also important to learn *what* is worth seeing through to the finish. Sometimes you may need to stop something in order to start something different. Being able to identify that a path has come to an end and it's time to start a new path is important. Finish the paths that are important to you.

Give Yourself the Gift of Risking Failure
The greatest opportunity to improve comes with finishing. This doesn't mean that you won't fail, but if you don't finish, you will never know. Failing can provide some of the greatest learning opportunities, and if you don't see it through, you will have missed the greatest gift of giving effort. Don't be afraid to finish and see the outcome. Stories aren't written about things people *almost* accomplished or had a good idea but never followed through. If it is important and you believe in it, do it the best you can, and if you care enough about it, finish.

3. Sustain Self-Discipline and Self-Motivation
We've seen that a key difference between athletes who set themselves apart from others is that they have *sustained* motivation that

comes from within and is applied to actions, discipline, sacrifices, and decisions that others aren't willing to make.

This motivation that wasn't created by a one-time preseason motivational speaker and gone a week later, not from a parent or coach that yells at you a few hours a day a few weeks a year—it's the person you're never without. It takes most of us years after our playing days are over to realize that what we get out of being athletes really is in our control. Being disciplined is really about your current self, looking out for your future self, and helping that person reach their goals.

Do you have what it takes? You do. It's inside of all of us. But do you have what it takes to bring that out of you and leave what you don't need behind. The hard part sometimes isn't what you'll have to do but stopping the things that are preventing you from reaching the next level of growth.

Look at those who have succeeded as athletes or even changed the world; they all had the ability to motivate themselves and stay disciplined over an extended period. Sometimes the difference between being average and being great is just what you choose to do when you're tired. It doesn't mean you don't need sleep, but throughout history humans that have been successful are those willing to work hard, push through when tired, make sacrifices, and make good decisions.

It's easy to work hard when someone is forcing you to, but when others go home or no one will ever know you took those extra reps, will you do it? Everyone has different sources of motivation, but the most successful athletes are those who aren't dependent on others for this.

The problem isn't typically a shortage of resources or YouTube videos you can watch on how to improve your agility, shooting, etc. It's finding the discipline to work on your craft day after day that most can't do. It's also easy to do your job when you're feeling good or when others are watching. Those who set themselves apart are disciplined enough to *sustain their own motivation*. Figure out what motivates you, what gives you that "chip" on your shoulder, and if you really want to be great, you have to be able to provide yourself with your own motivation, no one else.

Look closely at your habits. There is a lot of power in routine and creating *good* habits for yourself. Whether it's pregame, postgame, or during training, your brain knows your body better than you do, and if you create good habits, you will benefit without maybe even knowing. Being disciplined to keep these habits also allows you to spend more time on thinking about the important things.

Tip: Create the environment and systems around you that allow for the encouragement of discipline. This also means removing distractions and things you know will only make it harder.

Finding Your Fire: An Elite Athlete's Killer Instinct
The best athletes can find another gear—a trigger that kicks in and says, "Nope, you're not beating me." This is a killer instinct that even the nicest, calmest, most humble athlete can call upon and can be the difference between being a champion and just being average.

For most athletes, the thing to fear most isn't an injury or being cut—it's comfort. The well-known story of Muhammad Ali (Cassius Clay) getting his red bike stolen when he was twelve is an example of figuring out what can ignite the fire inside of you and remind you of what you're chasing and the motivation needed to keep going. Ali was introduced to the gym he began his boxing career in and his first coach because someone stole that bike. Six years later, he won the gold medal.

It doesn't have to be a stolen bike or a death, and it's possible to create that environment that gives you this fire. Ali was giving back, paying it forward, and using his platform to help others, current and future. (Note: Ali was known for his humanitarian efforts across the globe, and that will outlast any athletic achievements.)

Think about what caused you to want to play the sport you now play. Think of a time or situation where something that you worked hard for or cared about was taken away from you. And think about the impact what's happening now can have on your future and ability to take the path you want. Remember this trigger, learn how to control that emotion, and understand the appropriate times to use that fire. (Note: Someone else can't create this for you. It's you.)

4. Seek Ways to Set Yourself Apart

In order to get to places others can't, you must be willing to do what other people aren't. Show up early. Stay late. Do the extra. The only way to set yourself apart from everyone else is by doing what they are doing…and more. Just enough will keep us moving forward. Doing more will set us apart. A common mistake I see athletes make is just doing what everyone else is doing and expecting a different outcome than them or others willing to put in the "extra." It's not how it works.

What if everyone just followed what those before them did? We would be doing the same type of training from hundreds of years ago. At some point, someone decides that there is a better way—a way that will make them better than their opponent. This will also require you to actively seek ways to set yourself apart. Life will happily let you follow the mold of being normal or merely surviving. If you don't like it, don't accept it. Be observant, pay attention, and don't wait for someone to tell you to do it. The keys are creativity, timing, and the art of doing something even when you don't want to, without someone forcing you.

Tip: Adjusting routines and habits can be good but avoid changing too many things all at once. You're not going to know what helped or if something did what it was supposed to. You'll know best when and how to adapt, and don't underestimate making small changes in the right direction. Most people can't continue making small gains. Don't be like most people.

Follow the mold. Then break it. Earlier, we talked about tracking and using the experiences of others to guide our own path. Eventually, if you want to go where others haven't, you're going to have to break from the pack. Is there a way you can get more reps in the gym? Stay longer in the cage? Train longer than what people normally do at your school? If you could dream up the ideal-training scenario that you think would help you the most, what would it look like? Have you ever asked?

Learn to do things you don't want to. You're not alone in having times when you just really don't feel like waking up early and working out or getting extra shots in. That's normal; it's what most people do and why it's a great place to set yourself apart. If you wait for someone to come and hand it to you, prepare yourself for a long wait. It's not coming. Go after it. Do whatever you can to learn new techniques. Do more than the athlete next to you. Do something that not even you thought possible. If you want to be ordinary, do ordinary things. If you want to set yourself apart, it's going to take *extra* effort.

5. Moments of Impact: Identify and Embrace

A "moment of impact" is the moment that you spend all those hours in the weight room, waking up early in the winter, and making all your sacrifices for. It may come at a critical time in a game or years after your life as a young athlete is over. The key is to make sure you are physically and mentally ready for it. The harder you work, the more moments you will have to make a name for yourself, help those around you, and be a part of something people will never forget. Make the most of what you've got when you've got it.

> **"Seize the moment when the timing is right. There comes a special moment in everyone's life, a moment for which that person is born...when he seizes it, it is his finest hour."**
> —Winston Churchill

Train yourself for these moments. Imagine yourself in that moment before you get there. Be prepared, and don't just wait for someone to hand it to you. When that moment does come, be able to identify it and attack it. You don't know if you will get another one and won't want to have any regrets.

If you showed up, tried your best, and did whatever you could to prepare yourself for that moment, you have nothing to worry about. Don't wait for someone else to do it. Embrace the pressure; enjoy it. See an opportunity; seize it. Control your own destiny and live it to the fullest.

Regardless of outcome, you won't have any regrets if you did what you could to prepare and gave it your best effort. But if you're not ready or won't risk the chance of failure, you might. You'll have the respect of all past athletes if you just embrace your moment and do your best.

6. Surround Yourself with the *Right* People
One of the best things you can do in athletics and in life is to surround yourself with "the right" people. This doesn't mean the

smartest, the most athletic, or those who are the most like you. You don't always have the choice, but when you do, learn how to do it, and choose wisely.

The best teams, whether it's for a project in class or a world championship team, have a wide variety of people involved. You don't want everyone to be just like you. If they are, you're in trouble. As you get older, you realize that the more different you are, the easier the project may be and the better the outcome. The next time your teacher says, "Ok, find a group," if you're smart, you'll try to surround yourself with people with different strengths, not your buddies that are just like you.

Are you the kind of teammate you would want on your team? What can you do to do a better job of helping others head in the right direction with you? What do you bring to the table?

Life is too short to spend it with people who don't appreciate the time and energy you are willing to give them. If you find yourself with people who don't treat you as well as you'd like or are making you move further from your dreams rather than closer, move on.

It is important to have people around you who will push you and stretch your comfort zone, but that doesn't always mean it's the "right" kind. During the 2015 Masters Golf Tournament, Jordan Spieth was leading and talked about his plans for that night before his next round. He was going to surround himself with friends, play Ping-Pong, no golf talk, just be there. These were the "right" people for that situation. They should be considerate, understand your needs, and want to adapt in order to help you succeed. They helped him be ready for his moment of impact without pushing him. He would go on to win that tournament and the next.

One of Arnold Schwarzenegger's keys to success is to "ignore the naysayers." There will always be people telling you no, sharing reasons why things are not possible and you can't achieve them. Ignore them. Surround yourself with people who genuinely care and want to see you succeed.

Are you the type of person people should be surrounding themselves with? Try to be the "right" people for your friends, and work hard at identifying what that means and why.

7. Learn the Art of Risk-Taking

Anyone who has accomplished anything great did so because they were willing to take a risk.

This doesn't mean to seek ways to put your life in danger or be unsafe for no reason, but to have the willingness to try something that comes with the risk of failing. Stand up for what you believe in, push yourself to rise to new levels, and learn to identify times to take a chance. You will be rewarded. Ask yourself, "What's a bigger risk—taking it or what happens if you don't? This one, or being eighty and looking back at your decision not to do it?" Here are three tips for risk-taking:

1. **Seek Discomfort**: If you want to grow, it doesn't come from times of comfort. The best things are often those that can come out of the harshest environments, and that is the perfect environment to hone our risk-managing skills. Our first tendency is to avoid the things that make us feel uncomfortable or that we don't want to do, but we know that the more we put ourselves in uncomfortable, high-pressure situations, the more normal they will feel. This is a huge advantage for an athlete who wants to perform at their peak.
2. **Develop Your "Sense of Adventure"**: One of the costs of being distracted by technology (in my opinion) is losing

our innate ability to see what's happening around us and letting our instincts help us guide the way. As an example, everything is being designed to make our daily lives "easier," from backing up a car to finding your iPhone. The danger here is we're slowly losing our ability to manage risk, make decisions, and neglect what's given humans fulfillment from our earliest days. The long-term costs of this are to be determined; don't let easy restrict your own innate senses and skills.

3. **Learn to Calculate and Manage, Not Be Afraid Of:** If you fail, get back up and move forward. Never let the chance of failure prevent you from taking a chance. If there is no chance of failure, chances are you aren't taking a big enough risk. Sometimes not taking a risk can be the most dangerous thing you can do. If the risk you are taking impacts someone else, that's something you need to calculate. Learning how to manage and mitigate risk but not eliminate it from your life is key for athletes advancing through levels.

The world's greatest explorers, people you read books about, humans who have changed the course of history, agreed to take risks. Most people will pursue the safest path whenever possible. The best legends aren't written about people who played it safe. Animals have instincts about how and when to take risks, and so do we.

8. Build Perspective and Protect It

It can take a lifetime to build perspective of what's important, figure out the right amount to care about things, and understand the big picture. The key is to know that there is a land beyond this mountain and the next. You're important, but it's also not all about you, and what may seem like a big deal might not be what it appears.

"Increase Your Intuition": Perspective and experience can increase your intuition, something the best athletes possess but which takes time, work, and attention. An example of being intuitive would be when we watch athletes like Alexander Ovechkin play hockey; he just seems to find himself in the right place at the right time. It's more than speed and skill; he pays attention, he's intuitive, he can see the play happening before others, and it puts him in a position to succeed.

It's also important to *protect* that perspective you gain. Always remember what it is like right now as a young athlete, student, etc. It may take hard work, but that's nothing new to you. This is your perspective; it can change over time, but don't let others make their perspective yours. A common mistake I see athletes make is experiencing small amounts of success and forgetting what motivated them early on, losing the fire, and forgetting what it was that made them work so hard. Have a short-term memory for bad games or previous mistakes, figure out a way to remind yourself of what motivates you, and refuse to settle. Athletes are trained to and are good at being able to move on quickly and not dwell on mistakes, errors, and missed shots. But this often leaks into also forgetting the good things we've done and what we had to go through. Don't lose the perspective you earn by just going through things, good and bad.

Perspective is going to benefit you as an athlete, reduce anxiety during the big game, and make everything more enjoyable as well. If you are enjoying it, you will work harder, and we all know what happens when people work hard at something. From experience comes perspective, from perspective comes wisdom, from wisdom comes principles that define you, and living by these principles will be what defines you. Don't forget it along the way, and don't forget the *real* you.

Tip: An easy first step you can make is to start paying closer attention and reduce the distractions.

9. Form an Alliance with Adversity

If you want something good, you'll have to fight for it, put in the work, and do what others aren't willing to do. When you are faced with adversity, it is your opportunity to grow. If things are easy, there is little you can learn. Welcome tough times, and learn to embrace having to overcome challenges. In fact, maybe the more, the better. One day you will be more thankful for the hard times and your ability to overcome them than the good times. Anyone who has ever done anything worthwhile has encountered difficulties. Everyone has issues, find a way to overcome them, and be better because of it.

> **"The ultimate measure of a man is not where he stands in moments of comfort and convenience. But where he stands at times of challenge and controversy."**
> —Martin Luther King Jr. (1963)

In my junior year of high school, I tore my ACL and would miss both football and hockey seasons as I went through six months of rehab. I wasn't sure if I would be able to play sports again, much less run. It was devastating. I now look back and wouldn't trade that experience for the world. I learned more about who I was, I gained perspective on being grateful for the little things, and it helped me become more mentally tough, which I continue to benefit from twenty-five years later.

Life is not easy, and I don't believe the goal should be to make it easy. Just use the hard parts to make you tougher, and turn it into a positive. It's struggle that allows growth. Those that succeed in nature are those that can embrace change, harness it, and adapt faster than those around them. Regardless of how you define success, throughout history we have known that those who have risen to the top all share that they at some point overcame adversity. They had grit and welcomed things that were hard. It doesn't mean they were never afraid.

What you do when the times are tough will be what defines you. If you're struggling to decide what you should do or to keep moving forward, go to your own guiding principles. Form an alliance with an adversity, look forward to whatever challenges you may be presented with, and when you come out on the other side, you will be better because of it. People want to follow the brave, tough, and those with moral courage, not those who are the best at making things easy.

Tip: If easy allows you more time to do something hard, great. If it allows you to do less or nothing, avoid it. It's easy to get fooled by having easy things fix difficult problems. Examples would be like going to your phone because it distracts and makes you feel. It doesn't mean you can't have a phone, but you should know the "help" you're feeling is not real and won't last long. Things like going and getting a lift in, going for a run, meditating—these are hard things sometimes to find the motivation to do but will make you feel better because you are better and not masking what you're feeling. You have to learn how to identify and regulate your emotions. If you're sad, it's ok and normal; the goal isn't to be happy all the time. Appreciate adversity.

10. Know your job. Be All In.

> "The world meets nobody halfway, if you want it, you've got to take it."
> —Sylvester Stallone as Lincoln Hawk (*Over the Top*)

How bad do you want it? Go to the mirror. Look yourself in the eye, and ask yourself this question. Do this your entire life. If you decide it's just not that important to you, and this is ok, move on and find a way to spend your time and energy on something you can give 100 percent to.

Find that thing you are willing to pull an all-nighter working on, make sacrifices for, and will be proud to say that yes, I tried my best, and be proud regardless of outcome. The athletes coaches like best are those that are all in, mentally and physically. They are coachable, make others on the team better, and because they are all in and self-driven, they are often the best players.

If you want to be an athlete who will always be remembered, learn to be all in away from the field and when nobody's watching. Mowing the lawn, being a good family member, doing your history homework—if you are all in, people will remember *all* that you are.

The most successful teams (or even families) consist of people who know their jobs and do them. It can change from day to day, game to game, and if you don't like it, you don't have to do it forever, but it's important that you do the job asked of you to the best of your ability before you start demanding another. Good things happen to people who give 100 percent to the job tasked to them.

If you are unclear of your job or how you can contribute, you should ask. Taking care of your little sister, getting rebounds, protecting the blue line—the jobs will vary, but the importance will not.

There are few things more powerful and contagious than *genuine* enthusiasm. If you want to be a leader, have people follow you, and make a difference, find the thing that others can see how it lights up your face when you talk about it. You'll have no problem being all in.

11. Develop Dynamic Balance

> "Find out what it is you want and go after it as
> if your life depends on it.
> Why? Because it does."
> —Les Browne

If you want to be ordinary, seek balance. If you want to be great, develop dynamic balance.

Bellwood Rewinds is a generator service company located on the eastern coast of the United Kingdom. On their website, they define the difference between static and dynamic balance as follows: *"Static balance refers to the ability of a stationary on object to its balance. This happens when the object's center of gravity is on the axis of rotation. Whereas dynamic balance is the ability of an object to balance while in motion or when switching between positions"* (www.bellwoodrewinds.co.uk). Diesel generators have nothing in common with the lives of athletes, or do they? Both need to remain in motion; the key to success for both is keeping the center of gravity aligned while lots of different parts continue to move. Life isn't static; those that achieve greatness can master times of being off-balance.

Mathew Kelly wrote the book *Off Balance: Getting Beyond the Work-Life Balance Myth to Personal and Professional Satisfaction*. He shares that the goal for most really isn't balance but satisfaction, and to do that, imbalance in various levels will be necessary. Note: Satisfaction does not mean getting everything you want. And that's ok.

If you want to be great, you must be willing to put in the time, effort, and sacrifices beyond normal to achieve a goal—even if it creates some temporary imbalances. The key to thriving in these times is intelligent self-understanding. You must be able to push yourself so you know your limits and what growth feels like while still being able to keep your center of gravity (physical and emotional). This is where the magic lives.

What if those that changed the world listened to the people questioning their unorthodox use of time and energy on a specific task and pursued easy, safe, and balanced? If your goal is balance, what happens if you achieve it? Everything will be average, mediocre? Keep moving; strive for more than just balance. There's nothing wrong with balance, but nothing great has ever come from it.

12. Give Back. Pay it Forward.
Someday you will have the chance to give back to the sport that you love, the community you grew up in, and help other athletes that will be in the same place you are in now. Paying it forward, doing something to help another, is the sincerest form of showing your gratitude and continuing the principles that were instilled into you. It's important that you continue this pattern.

Steve, the father of my friend Adam mentioned earlier in the book, would talk often about the importance of this and showed it through his actions. In the winter he would drive in from his farm in the country to meet us at the small gym in the middle school to take batting practice. We ran sprints in the dark in the hallways, hit tattered baseballs from an erratic, old pitching machine, and just spent time in the same place. Did the reps and sprints set me apart from others? Maybe, at the most, it played a small part, but the time spent in the same place, the sacrifices he made for us, and contributing to the building of habits and an environment for us to work hard, I still benefit from.

We don't want young athletes choosing to retire at the age of five after a fun year of T-ball to give back to the community, but you can get in the habit of donating old gloves, bats, etc., as you outgrow them. It should just be "what we do." Seek ways to show through your actions that you appreciate what someone has done for you. You will never regret acting on an opportunity to help someone, and you never know the impact it may have. If you want to thank a coach or your parents for what they have done or will do for you, do the same for another.

When I moved to Hawaii to coach with the baseball team at Hawaii Pacific University, Coach Les Akeo went out of his way to make me feel welcome at HPU and in Hawaii. He was one of the all-time best baseball players at HPU and one of only two baseball players in the athletic Hall of Fame. He is still highly respected in the community and runs the Pilikoko Baseball Clinic every year. The cost is an optional donation of canned goods. Coach Les has a unique combination of confidence and a demanding approach of his players, but he'd also pull over to fix your tire and welcome you into his house. Some would call it the aloha spirit, but the Akeos live it.

What number did Les Akeo have on his jersey when he played? Of course, 22. Find ways to give back and pay it forward, and those that follow will do the same. It's just what you do.

13. Enjoy the Process

When talking to former young athletes, coaches, and others that have been around the lives of young athletes, the most common response is "enjoy it." Enjoy the process, the practices, the time with teammates, the extra running, the good and the bad—find ways to embrace and enjoy it.

As a young athlete, I put a lot of pressure on myself. I wanted to do well and make others proud; what I didn't realize then was that all I really controlled was the process. And ultimately, it was the best part about being an athlete: experiencing the process with my friends and teammates. It wasn't all fun and trophies, and it shouldn't be. Important: Don't confuse "enjoying" things with more goofing around and not focusing. It's an art of timing that you have to learn. Things happen you can't control, but how you respond is in your control. In the spring of 2020, sports seasons around the world were cut short due to the Coronavirus. This wasn't an outcome anyone could have predicted or had control over, and although it's uncommon, it won't be the last disruptive event.

Being an athlete will be a process of good and bad, easy and hard. We often put too much pressure on expectations and not enough focus on the process. This is something you have control over. Take this important skill and apply it in your life, within sports and beyond.

14. If You Want to Be Anything, Timing is Everything

Self-motivation, hard work, and having the skills needed to help you on your quest are important, but they will all be in vain if your timing is off. The great ones have mastered it, and so can you. In nature we see an example of the importance of timing when it comes to migration. The survival of a species is often interconnected with others by their timing syncing up. If the timing gets thrown off, if someone isn't ready, if everyone isn't paying attention, everything gets disrupted.

Timing is important in nature, sports, and life, and for those on a quest for greatness, it's critical. You need to work hard to understand the right time to push, rest, when to read books, when to train hard, when to be selfish, when to serve, when to care, when not to, and even when to stop. You can definitely take cues and learn from those around you, but it's also got to be something you take ownership of and be responsible for. It's more than just hitting a shot at the buzzer; it's mastering the skill of "when." You must be agile enough to capitalize when the time is right and smart enough to know when to wait.

Learn to Have *Predator Patience*
In the wild, a predator has to know "when" to be patient if it wants to survive. Waiting in the weeds for their moment to strike, they are calm but still alert. It's important to be patient but also know when to act. Our prey are not small animals but moments of opportunity. If you miss them, your passion might starve. If you are too patient, you might never leave the weeds and could lose your hunger forever. Either option doesn't end well for someone hunting for excellence. Be patient but always ready. Achieving greatness is also going to take courage and being ok with the chance of failure. Predators fail more times than they succeed, but they know they have to try and try and try again. Learning from past mistakes helps them hone their craft and be ready for the next. Be brave; if you really want it, don't be afraid to go after it; you will be rewarded.

It's common to see athletes who have the right intentions but aren't moving with enough urgency. The moment of impact you've worked so hard to get an opportunity for is getting close; make sure you're ready and know that you are in control of mastering the time you are given.

Tip: Don't wait for everything to be "perfect." There's no such thing; a common mistake athletes make is waiting for the exact right time to do something. This is another example where you have to use your best judgment, learn from those around you, and don't let an opportunity pass. If things don't go exactly as planned, don't let it defeat you; give yourself some grace, not excuses.

15. Improve Your Input; Improve Your Output

Your body is your one and only vehicle you get. Sometimes you can make repairs, but without the proper fuel, data, and continuous upgrades to your internal computer, it's impossible to reach your maximum potential. Here are a few of the key inputs that are critical to the success of an elite athlete's output:

1. **Nutrition**: It's simple—the better you fuel yourself, the better you can perform. Keep an eye on the latest research, don't fall victim to trends, and learn what types of food you should eat and even *when*. You'll be a better athlete, and your body will thank you for it down the road. For more detailed nutritional advice, visit the TM22 website.
2. **Wisdom**: People are eager to share their advice. This can be extremely valuable or providing you with input that is hurting your output. Spend time around people that you know are genuine and care about the person you are beyond the court.
3. **Rest and Recovery**: An adequate amount of rest, sleep, and time for your body to recover is critical. Your body and mind can't operate at full capacity without it, and sustained amounts of deprivation can result in a variety of negative health effects. The key is figuring out the difference between knowing when your body needs to rest and when you need to push through. No two athletes are the same; learn what your body needs and do it.
4. **Intellectual Data**: You have an internal computer that is being programmed by what you give it. Books, speakers, classes, and taking the time to look at research will tell your computer how you want it to operate. If all it receives is mind-numbing videos, that's the output you're going to get, and you were the one that programmed it.

5. **Spiritual**: In this context, I am not using spiritual as the same as being religious. Regardless of what you believe in or don't believe in, I believe everyone has a spirit, a soul, a thing inside that you only you know and cannot be taken from you. People feed their spirit in lots of different ways—meditating, talking, listening, and helping others. The more positivity you can provide it, the more positivity you provide to those around you.

Note on training your brain: You are what you think. If you can master the mental side of being an athlete, you will experience benefits that can set you apart not just in sports but in the rest of your life.

Positive thought makes us better athletes, but this reaches far beyond the playing field. She shares that when we are sick, our brain signals fatigue to our body so that it can get the time and energy devotion it needs to fight a virus. The same feeling of fatigue applies when the brain first detects harm to our body. It isn't our muscles, lungs, or heart that are the first to tell our bodies to slow down. It's the brain. Be mindful of what and how you think about things. Give time and attention to mastering the mental side of sports, positive visualization, and imagine yourself in pressure situations during training so your brain is prepared for the desired response.

Tip: Athletes are fortunate to have learned how good taking care of your body can feel and the impact it can have on your mind. If you don't play sports, it's hard to know what to do in the weight room; those habits don't exist, and it's a much harder thing to just "start" later in life. Take advantage of this. You get what you put in; be mindful of what you're putting into your mind, body, and the environment around you.

16. Unleash the Power of Sacrifice

> "More people have the talent than you would think. Few are willing to make the necessary sacrifices."
> —Matthew Kelly, *Off Balance: Getting Beyond the Work-Life Balance Myth to Personal and Professional Satisfaction*

You can't achieve greatness without the willingness to make sacrifices along the way. A lot of people say they want to be great; few are willing to do what it takes and make the sacrifices. Sacrifices shouldn't include things like your family, character, or treating others with respect, but they could include things like how you spend your free time and the number of distractions you allow yourself, and, if done properly, it will be one of the best ways you can set yourself apart.

When I was growing up, my dad worked at University of Minnesota-Waseca until the early '90s when it was shut down and turned into a prison. For the next seventeen years, he would commute over an hour each way to work. Never once did he tell me no when I asked him to play catch when he got home. It would be years until I realized the sacrifice he was making for me as an athlete and for my family as a father. I don't remember the advice he gave me about throwing a baseball those nights, but I do remember the lesson of sacrifice he provided. It's not easy to make sacrifices sometimes, and this is good. Use this to set yourself apart.

17. True Confidence: Find It, Grow It, and Share It

Everyone knows how important confidence is for athletes. Me telling you to just be more confident is about as effective as when someone is yelling "Relax!" or "Focus!" at you from the stands. I've never met an athlete who found that helpful. You hear it at every game.

Confidence comes from self-belief; self-belief comes from self-awareness. Knowing your weaknesses, your strengths, what you've overcome, how hard you've worked, and your ability to accomplish the task in front of you, these are things that only the athlete knows and is responsible for reminding themselves of. "True" confidence will bring you a sense of calm and composure and the capacity to give yourself the best shot at succeeding.

There is a fine line between being confident and arrogant. A confident athlete believes in themselves but is still humble, still listens, and is still a good teammate. An arrogant athlete has an exaggerated view of their abilities, often masking insecurities, and hopes that bragging about how good they think they are will carry them over the top. But this arrogance won't provide the same sense of calm, composure, or capacity, and no one will want to be around you.

As a young athlete, I can remember finding my first levels of confidence from others, both from seeing their confidence and from believing in me before I did. It unleashed an inner self-confidence, as if I were given approval to do so. Surrounding yourself with the right people is a great way to improve confidence and a reminder that you can have the same impact on others.

You may have heard of the fake-it-'til-you-make-it approach. This is a self-belief that maybe doesn't fully exist yet, but you feel the need to show others in order to get where you want to be. The problem with this approach is the impact it has on developing "true" self-belief and ultimately confidence. You will know if you're lying to yourself, and that creates some bad mental habits.

How to Grow Confidence
Positive self-talk, visualization, remembering all the work you've put in, and good plays you've made—the more experience you

have accomplishing the task at hand, the more prepared you'll feel. Even if that means shooting baskets in your driveway, you can tell your mind that it matters. Most athletes can remember mistakes, errors, and shots missed much more than good plays. Make it a habit of noting things you've done well, mentally or physically, and you don't need to post them on social media. This is for you.

Important: You can be both humble and confident. Athletes with true confidence know how to listen, be good teammates, and share their self-belief in others.

The Power of Self-Belief
Once on a trip through Alaska, I stopped at a small shack along the side of the road. An older gentleman was selling pictures he had taken of various animals, mountains, trees, etc. On the wall of his small shack studio, he had many pictures with red ribbons. They were all second-place ribbons, and when I asked him about them, he said that he had never won any competitions, just lots of second-place entries and below. There is nothing wrong with second place, but the fact that the guy didn't let his lack of winning discourage him from believing in the beauty of his photos or his own self-confidence made his pictures just that much cooler. I bought several of his photos. Believe in yourself, and others will too. Sometimes this means breaking the attachment with the person you used to be.

Every athlete goes through periods of self-doubt. We often quickly dismiss the things we did well and dwell on mistakes. The problem is that this can lead to a lack of confidence and impact your ability to perform at a high level. What you believe in is going to change, but one thing that can never change is believing in yourself. It doesn't mean you can't have faith in other things, but never lose it in yourself. Even in the times of failure, you want to at least be able to feel like you were yourself. There is nothing worse than trying to pretend to be something you're not; things go wrong, and then if you knew if you had just been yourself, everything would have been much better.

There is only one you. You have strengths and unique gifts that no one else on this planet has. It's ok to be unique. It's ok to be different. If someone doesn't like the way you are, don't waste your time and energy being around that person. Put trust in yourself, that is the person you can trust most in this world, and you should for good reason. Make your name the one that others want to be, and give everything you have to be the best version of yourself, no matter how weird you might be. Your greatest enemy can be self-doubt, and your greatest ally is self-belief.

> **"The bad news: You are not going to fit in with everyone. The good news: The great ones never do."**
> —Unknown

Stand Up for Yourself

I think it can feel easier to stick up for others than ourselves. But if you let the world take advantage of you, it will. Standing up for yourself and being able to self-advocate doesn't make you arrogant, selfish, or disrespectful—there's a way to do it that will make people respect you more. It takes courage; others can help, but you're the only one who can stand up for yourself. Don't get pushed around for something you really want and regret it later.

I see athletes get taken advantage of because of their culture, gender, or just not being assertive enough at times or worrying about how it will be perceived. Examples include things like getting time on the court, reps in the cage, getting skipped in line for a squat rack, an opportunity at showcases, and even how they talk to a college coach, asking how their season is going. Step up; be confident; you've put in the work. If you don't stand up for yourself, the result could be someone less deserving of getting the things you've worked so hard to get.

I've seen situations where the "nice" athlete or parents who are "understanding" get taken advantage of while another athlete who is willing to complain will rise above. There's a balance between being the athlete who stands up for themselves and can self-advocate and the athlete who complains about everything. There isn't a magic button here, and add it to the list where being aware, having courage, and using good judgment is key.

Tip: You also need to know that not getting what you want is both possible and could be good for you. Either outcome is dependent upon your reaction to it. This is easy for me to say, and you've probably heard your parents say it, but it's good to not always get what you want.

Learn to Be the Right You at the Right Times

Miyamoto Musashi is credited for the famous Chinese saying, "It's better to be a warrior in a garden than a gardener in a war," which gets at what an elite athlete should strive for. It's important to train hard, be strong, and equip yourself with the skills needed in sports and life but also have humility and self-control, and don't find yourself being weak and ill prepared for the challenge.

You should always "be yourself," but understand that there are different situations that need different "versions" of you. For example, there are times when you need to be responsible, empathetic, or calm, and others that need the energetic, aggressive, or maybe even "crazy" you.

You know those different versions, and since you know yourself better than anyone, it's your responsibility. On the field, you should be fierce, confident, and brave; off the field, humble, respectful, and open-minded; and, at home, caring and patient. Stick to the core values and principles you stand for; believe in yourself, current and future; and never let self-doubt pull you down. If you don't believe in yourself, no one else will. Be yourself. Trust that person. Stand up for them.

18. Show Character through *Genuine* Action

> "The voyage of the best ship is a zigzag line of a hundred tacks. See the line from a sufficient distance, and it will straighten itself to the average tendency. Your genuine action will explain itself and will explain your other genuine actions."
> —Ralph Waldo Emerson, "Self-Reliance" (1841)

The key word here is *genuine*. If you want to see someone's true character, watch what they do, not what they say. We all know someone who is really good at saying the right thing but doesn't "walk the walk." Don't just say the right things; do the right things. Doing the right thing for your team when things maybe aren't going well for you is difficult but critical. Don't be the "front-runner," who is a great teammate when things are going well for them but an energy sucker when they're struggling. Be consistent.

Simply just saying you want to be successful won't get you very far. It takes hard work, sacrifice, and a willingness to do lots of small actions to get you there. You should find comfort in the fact that you don't have to worry about always saying the right things to get where you want to go. Lead by example; show through your actions what is important to you; your teammates and coaches will see that and remember it far longer than the athlete who could "talk the talk."

If they were going to create a scholarship in your name, right now, what would it embody? (Remember, it would be a reflection of not only what you have accomplished but also what you want to see happen. Do your present actions reflect those traits? If not, it's not too late.)

You can have an impact on a lot of people. If you say the wrong thing or make a mistake, just remember that it's a collection of your genuine actions over an extended period that people will remember and that show your true character.

19. Invest Wisely with Your Time and Energy

If you want future success, make the investment now. If you wait until the future arrives to start doing things differently, it's too late—someone else will get that success.

Besides maybe your health, time may be the most valuable thing you have—protect it. Your energy meter will continue to diminish throughout life. Investing wisely now is like making an investment in your future self. Investments are typically tricky, but an investment in yourself is an easy decision and one you have to make.

You only get a certain amount of time and energy each day. Don't waste it worrying about what others think or with those who don't appreciate it. Find the right combination of having fun but also continuing to improve as an athlete and person. Do the things you don't love in moderation; get addicted to fulfilling your passion. If something is "really" important to you, you'll make the time.

> "Great minds discuss ideas. Average minds discuss events. Small minds discuss people."
> —Eleanor Roosevelt

There are two kinds of people, energy givers and energy takers. Be an energy giver. The next time you find yourself "passing the time," just remember you're never going to get that time back. Are you sure you want to spend it doing that? You also need to learn how to use time as an ally that can allow you to recover, not an enemy that, when used poorly, can tear you down.

Warning: A common tendency of success-driven athletes is to spread themselves too thin. Learn to identify what you need when you need it, and don't be afraid to follow through. At the end of the day, only you truly know what you need.

The TM22 athlete follows the definition of leadership that includes identifying the needs of everyone in the group and doing what it takes to succeed. But you can't do that if you aren't taking care of yourself first. Sometimes being selfish is the best way to help others, and you have to be wise about taking care of yourself as much as you do others.

A note on technology: It isn't going anywhere. You can own it; just don't let it own you. The debate on technology is not if it's good or bad—that's determined by the discipline of the user.

For many it has become one of the biggest distractions and kidnappers of time and energy. Social media and reels are designed to make you spend hours mindlessly scrolling. Do you know how many movies, books, and legends are written about people who spend their lives distracted by technology? Zero. Being silent is ok. Being alone is ok. Not being constantly entertained or informed of what your friends are up to is ok. Just "being" doesn't make you weird. Set yourself apart by disconnecting from this distraction; use it effectively and only in moderation.

20. Take Ownership of Your Own Development

> "Destiny is not a matter of chance. It is a matter of choice.
> It is not a thing to be waited for, it
> is a thing to be achieved."
> —William Jennings Bryan

No one gets to the top alone, it's important to be able to ask for help, but the best athletes also know that they have to take ownership of their own development, internal and external.

If you want to set yourself apart, there's a lot you can do that doesn't depend on who your coach is, what lessons your parents can afford, or even if there's a global pandemic. You need to take responsibility for finding ways to improve on your own, most won't, and this is why it's so important. It is your job to motivate yourself, no one else's.

What can you do, in addition to what your coach or parents tell you to do? What happens if they don't know you as well as you do? Don't want it as badly? There's a growing number of online resources, training videos, and other ways that you can take it upon yourself to improve that no one else has ever even thought of. Don't wait for someone to tell you to do it; take it into your own hands. It should also feel good to know that your path isn't up to anyone but you. If your coach isn't the greatest, it doesn't matter; learn what you can, be a good teammate, and keep growing.

This development also extends beyond athletics. You have no way of knowing when or how, but if you do it right, your experiences as a young athlete can help you the rest of your life.

Taking Ownership Requires Toughness

Those with the most mental toughness and perseverance are those who will be successful in athletics and in life. Being a young athlete can be tough; life can be tough; keep fighting and keep moving forward, no matter what. It is your choice which direction you want to go; don't wait for someone else to make you that choice for you. What sets apart the greats is that they were able to self-motivate when times were tough. It's also important to understand what it really means to be "tough."

You can see lots of examples of "being tough" in sports, and it's a great place to grow your toughness, but I really didn't understand what true toughness was until I was done competing. As you get older and as your parents get older, things in life become more complicated, and you will need toughness you never knew you had. Playing in the fourth quarter of a tight game requires toughness, but that's nothing close to what you will have to have later in life. When I now think of tough, I think of my grandma raising a lot of kids, crops, and animals on a farm with a prosthetic leg. Keep your eyes open to what other people are going through, learn from it, and use it to increase your own innate toughness. It's in there; you may just need to identify it and bring it out.

Can You Make Yourself Tougher?

I think so—part of it comes from having perspective, being disciplined, and also understanding toughness can be revealed in different forms. James Loehr, a sports psychologist, wrote a great book, *The New Toughness Training for Sports*. He reveals a series of exercises you can do to help draw out your innate toughness and better prepare yourself mentally, physically, and emotionally. Being tough essentially is the ability to operate at a high capacity emotionally, mentally, and physically when you're not feeling well, you're tired, things don't go as planned, and you must adapt, or all the above. Loehr refers to this peak feeling as your "Ideal Performance State." The longer you can be in it, the more you can dominate.

Don't let anyone prevent you from growing your toughness. When someone tries to make an excuse for you, or you make one for yourself, you are actually robbing yourself neurologically from improving from that challenge. Be accountable, find ways to motivate yourself, and your "true" toughness will grow. As hard as adversity can be, if you learn to harness it and the lessons it provides, it will gift you with some new "true" toughness you can benefit from the rest of your life. Whether it's your mental toughness or developing into your maximum potential, you will regret it if you come up short and leave it in someone else's hands. Take ownership and take advantage of the opportunity to determine your own destiny.

Tip: Something I see the best athletes willing to do again and again is just having the willpower to do the things they don't want to do without someone having to force them. It's not that they don't get tired or have endless energy; they've just taken ownership of their own discipline, motivation, and development as an athlete.

21. Become a Master of Preparation

> "If I had six hours to chop down a tree, I'd spend the first four hours sharpening the axe."
> —Abraham Lincoln

It's critical that you learn the importance of proper preparation in the right amounts and in the right way. Mentally and physically, figuring out what is best for you in that situation is an elite athlete trait. Playing the actual game can be the easy (and should be the fun) part; it's the time preparing for your moment of impact and doing the small things that will get you where you need to be.

Optimize the Present; Design Your Own Future
Whatever *it* currently is won't always be. That isn't the most grammatically sound sentence, but a reminder to both enjoy things while you can and, if things aren't, good don't worry—they'll change. The people who are most successful, happy, and satisfied in sports (and in life) are those who can optimize their current situation. No matter how bad or how much you'd rather be doing something else or how it just really isn't ideal, you have to find a way to optimize your current situation.

Optimize: to make the best or most effective use of (a situation, opportunity, or resource).

Making the best of the current situation doesn't just mean accepting that things should stay this way but taking control of its impact on you. You're on a long car ride with your family, you're on your tenth stroke of the hole, you're missing out on a tournament, you need surgery and will be out five months—none of these situations may feel ideal, and you're probably right, but you have to figure out a way to make the best of it. There is good that comes out of any situation. Ask yourself how you can optimize your present situation, current job, or current body. If you can live with the idea that you just always have to optimize your current situation, it will lead to better ones and prepare you for the ones you dreamed about.

If you just expect it to happen or leave it to "destiny," it's probably not going to come. You've got to create that path and take it. Do what you can with what you have and prepare your mind for when chance appears. Learn to optimize.

The Power of Self-Simulation

One of the best things you can do to prepare yourself for high-pressure, high-stakes moments is to self-simulate. Put yourself in those moments where everything is on the line before you get there. If you go bowling, imagine a scout standing behind you and your scholarship is riding on you getting that last pin; you're at the park shooting hoops and you picture the whole season riding on you making the next shot; you're playing darts at your friend's house; you hit the bullseye and your team wins; miss and you lose. Your brain and body will be so used to that feeling of pressure and increased heart rate that when the time really comes, you'll be ready.

Of course it's important to be present: it's all you can control, but the best athletes know that the outcome of the event, the showcase, is often determined months in advance by how you train.

Physically and mentally, visualize that moment, what it will feel like, how badly you want it, and what it will take. Most people wait until the night before or until they find out what that event is; the best athletes have been thinking about the "potential" of that moment months, if not years, in advance. Give yourself enough time and space to prepare. Find a routine. Stick to it. It will pay off.

22. Outwork Everyone Else

If you really want something, you've got to work hard; there's no other option. If you only choose one of the twenty-two lessons included in this chapter, choose this one. Nothing great has ever been achieved by half-heartedly going through the motions.

Your hard work must include consistency and intelligent effort. Working out hard for ten hours one day and taking the rest of the week off isn't going to work. It's working hard, day after day, doing the small things the right way even without anyone telling you to do it.

The bad news is that if you don't work hard in deciding your future, those who did work hard will decide it for you. The good news is that it's all in your control. If you outwork everyone else, it will set you apart, and all your hard work will be worth it. Show up earlier and stay late; run harder and hustle more; and show through your actions and hard work that you are an athlete on his or her way to the top. You may not have control over your DNA or talent, but you do control how hard you work. *Everything is earned; you're not entitled to anything. If you want it, work hard.*

The older you get, the smarter you will have to be about *how* you work hard. Maximizing time, effort, and resources could be what sets you apart from others, even if you work just as hard.

> "There is no substitute for hard work."
> —Thomas Edison

Be a Relentless Acquirer of Knowledge

Most athletes understand that, if you want to excel, it will require a lot of time in the gym, training, running, sweating, and going through what most of us picture when we hear the word *grinding*. But another crucial difference we see between an average athlete and the one that sets getting ahead as their goal is their ability to not just work hard in the weight room but to do whatever it takes to keep learning, asking questions, and acquiring knowledge—they can never know enough.

Whether you're being forced to read this book or you took it upon yourself to learn from other athletes, you're here now. If you're trying to get the best out of yourself, you can't be ashamed of wanting to keep learning, and you can't be worried about being labeled a "try hard." Whatever it is that you decide to do and that you're passionate about, be relentless about wanting to acquire more knowledge and be open-minded about learning new things. Don't be the know-it-all athlete. We all know that guy/girl who, even at a young age, has been told everything they need to know and have ended listening to anyone outside their circle. Oh, you had good coaches—cool. Your club coach played pros—good for them. Your dad played and was the best in town, and he taught you—awesome. Elite athletes never stop learning and trying to acquire more knowledge, advice, and new ways of doing things. This will require some humility. You get what you put in; people get what they deserve. Work hard. You won't regret it.

The Summit Awaits

Like most things in life, how you choose to use the lessons and skills included in this chapter will be what you make it. They aren't designed to eliminate others, make you agree with everything, or even provide shortcuts. It's more about trying to help you create the right systems, better perspectives, and make choices that can help you, if you choose to make them.

My hope is that you'll treat this as a collection that you can add to and create your own, and the goal isn't to implement every one of these tomorrow, but if you even do just one of these things, it will help you on your journey.

In the next chapter, we'll talk about the small-but-difficult distance that exists between elite athletes and reaching their goals and what you can do to take control of that environment.

The Athlete Outpost
Twenty-Two Key Skills and Lessons Critical to Your Quest

1. Make a Plan: The Power of Forecasting
2. Learn to Finish the Things that Matter
3. Sustain Self-Discipline and Self-Motivation
4. Seek ways to Set Yourself Apart
5. Moments of Impact: Identify and Embrace
6. Surround Yourself with the *Right* People
7. Learn the Art of Risk-Taking
8. Build Perspective and Protect It
9. Form an Alliance with Adversity
10. Know Your Job. Be All In.
11. Develop Dynamic Balance
12. Give Back. Pay It Forward.
13. Enjoy the Process
14. If You Want to Be Anything, Timing is Everything
15. Improve Your Input; Improve your Output
16. Unleash the Power of Sacrifice
17. True Confidence in Yourself: Find It, Grow It, Share It
18. Show Character through *Genuine* Action
19. Invest Wisely with Your Time and Energy
20. Take Ownership of Your Own Development
21. Become a Master of Preparation
22. Outwork Everyone Else

22—A GUIDE FOR YOUNG ATHLETES

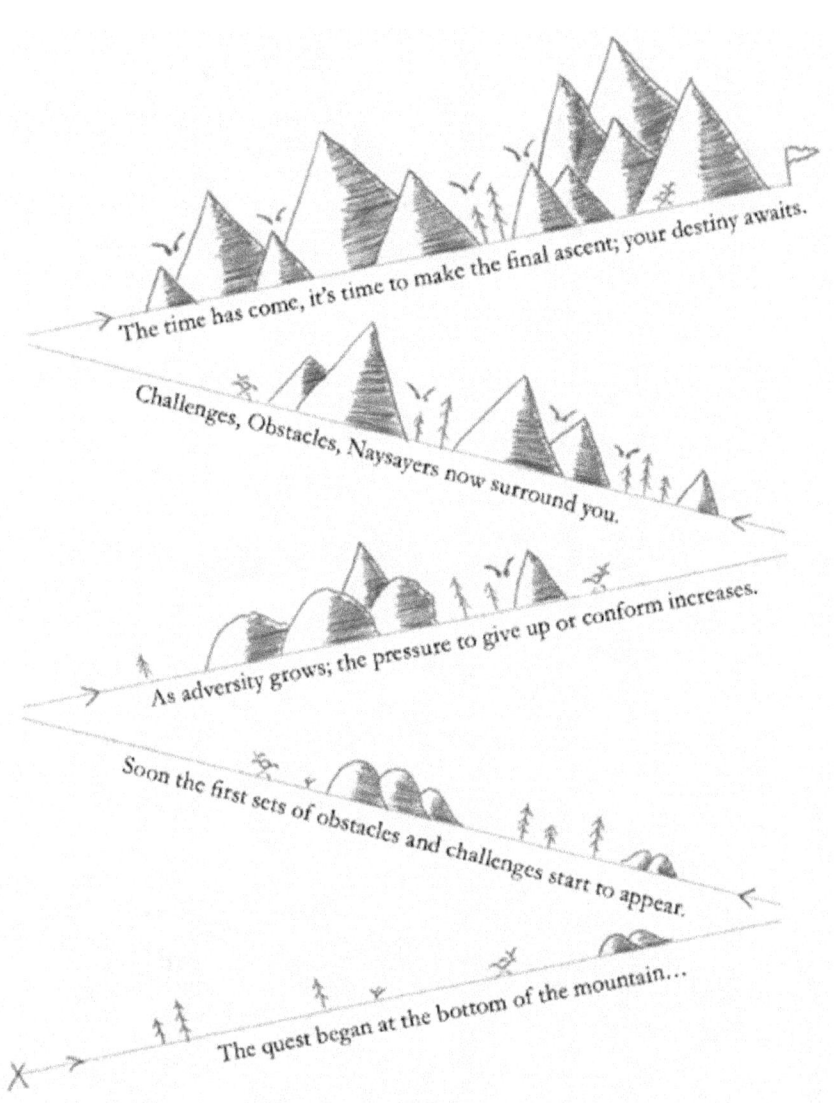

6

THE FINAL ASCENT

This is the distance that remains between you and what you've worked so hard to get. It's a lonely, difficult place, and it's where many athletes end their journey. This is the "final ascent."

The final ascent in this metaphor is the young athlete's mountain, but it's really the last bit of distance between you and your goals. It's the hardest stretch, and most will stop. This section of your life as a young athlete requires you to have the courage to do something different, do the things most are not willing to do, and do it without someone standing there telling you what to do and when to do it. This will require discipline and drive you never knew you had, which is why creating the right systems, habits, routines, and small day-to-day actions are so important. All great athletes, regardless of the help they did or did not have, had to at some point say, "All right, it's up to me to do the work to make this happen and finish what I started." If you can find the discipline to finish this final, difficult stretch, it will also prove all those who didn't believe in you wrong.

As you enter the area that stands between you and your goals, whenever that might be, you may get an uneasy feeling and an urge to regain the path that all others are on. You've got to decide not to give in to self-doubt or be fooled by the attraction of comfort. The realm you are about to enter is not easy; most won't understand the discipline, sacrifices, and drive required because they've never been there. But you'll be ready.

Beware: People are going to start to try to categorize you into things *they* are familiar with. It's what they know. It will seem off to them for you to be pursuing more than they did. Don't give up on what you know you can do just because they didn't. If you keep going and do what you can to reach your goals, even if you don't get there, you'll sleep well knowing you control your own destiny. Most don't have the courage to make this choice; just "hoping" isn't enough.

The following chapter will address some specific ways you can begin to take action to create the systems and environment for the right habits to occur during this important stretch. The result will be an opportunity to set yourself apart, let your genuine action show where you intend to go, and venture to places you never thought possible. Don't worry about how your story started; it's how it ends that matters. Regardless of the outcome, regardless of what you're trying to finish or achieve, you'll at least know you made the effort and can leave any regrets behind.

The Man in the Arena

"It is not the critic who counts; not the man who points out how the strong man stumbles, or where the doer of

deeds could have done them better. The credit belongs to the man who is actually in the arena, whose face is marred by dust and sweat and blood; who strives valiantly; who errs, who comes short again and again, because there is no effort without error and shortcoming; but who does actually strive to do the deeds; who knows great enthusiasms, the great devotions; who spends himself in a worthy cause; who at the best knows in the end the triumph of high achievement, and who at the worst, if he fails, at least fails while daring greatly, so that his place shall never be with those cold and timid souls who neither know victory nor defeat."
—Theodore Roosevelt, *Citizenship in a Republic*
(April 23, 1910)

(Elite athletes appreciate competition and respect athletes going to battle, regardless of the team they play for.)

The *Nature* of the Young-Athlete Mountain

Mountains can be dissected into zones. One of the key players that determines the nature of the zone is the "elevational impact." At certain elevations, some things can just no longer grow, the conditions are too harsh, and only the most resilient, toughest living creatures can survive.

Altitudinal Zonation (Nature)
The natural layering of ecosystems due to environmental conditions

Athlete Zonation (Athletes)
The natural layering of athletes who are willing to do what it takes or not.

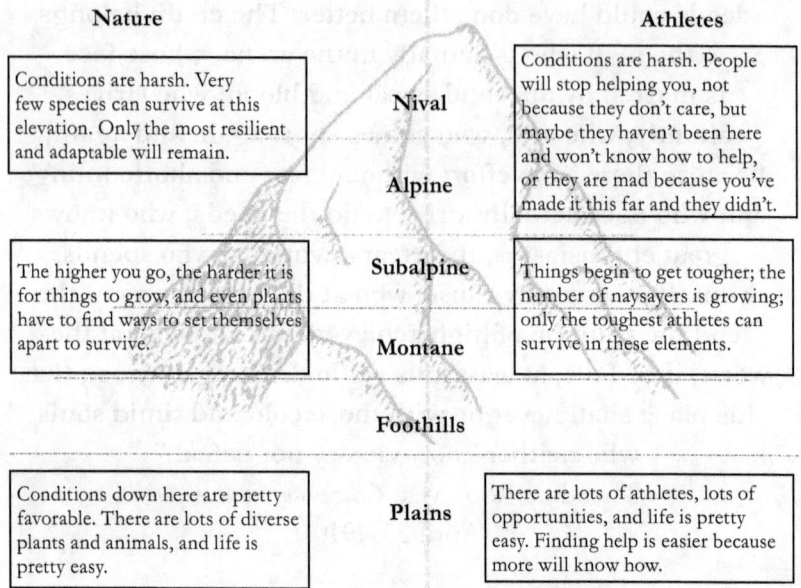

Tip: You can prepare yourself for this climb by using a skill known as "base camping." Along your journey, the more you can put yourself into tough environments, the more you can normalize pressure situations and adversity, and the changing conditions will feel easier as a result. Create the systems, routines, and habits around you that will enable the results you're working for.

Ten Ways to Impact the Systems and Environment around You

A lot of things are out of our control—but not everything. The goal should be to create an environment around you that has systems in place to help you get to whatever that "final ascent" might be. Here are some ways you can impact these systems.

1. Identify Real Sacrifices and Know When to Make Them.

You know by now the importance of making sacrifices if you want to set yourself apart. But what does that look like? Being on your phone for nine hours instead of ten is not really a sacrifice, nor is refusing to mow the lawn because you are in season and want to save your legs.

Your family, your health, and your principles are nonnegotiable; nothing is more important than these. Look at some of the ways you spend your time right now and ask yourself if they are standing between you and your dreams. Could it be spent in a better way? It doesn't mean you don't ever watch TV again, but maybe during this critical time, you make the sacrifice of working out or reading a book instead. It won't be easy, but how bad do you want it?

If your friends are mad at you for not hanging out with them one weekend, it's ok; they will eventually understand, and if they don't, maybe they weren't worth spending time with anyway.

2. Ask for Help: Know *When* and *How* to Do It.

We sometimes confuse being brave and having courage with never asking for help. If you want to be successful, you have to ask for help. People love being asked for their help and advice. It shows you value their opinion, and what you get back will be extremely important in continuing to move forward.

Seek help from parents, coaches, teachers, friends, and anyone you feel can help you along your path. Asking for help is a sign of both courage and respect. (Note: this is not help in the form of picking up your dirty clothes or doing your chores for you.) Questions like, "Hey, Coach, I was just wondering if you could teach me some more drills I can do on my own?" or "Hey, Mr. Ginther, I'm having trouble with what we covered this past week; do you have a few minutes to help me?" or "Hey, Mom, I see how hard you're working to help me pursue my dreams. How can I help *you*?"

Sometimes the best person to ask for help is you. If you ever feel in a rut, go for a walk. Ask yourself what is wrong and what is right; is it something you can control? If yes, pick one thing to do. Going for a walk doesn't make you weird—I promise.

Tip: Don't wait until it's too late. If you're having trouble fielding a ground ball, making free throws, or balancing school and sports, ask for help; the worst thing that can happen is that the person can say no and you seek other ways. Be sincere; help can come from the most unexpected places.

3. Build Good Habits. Set Yourself up for Success.

You walk into class on the first day of school, and every seat is open. The teacher says, "Sit wherever you want." If you want to be great, do *not* sit in the seats in the back.

You don't have to sit front and center, but just don't sit in the back. Nothing says I don't care, I don't respect what you're going to say, or I'm just going to goof off, like placing yourself in the back row. It seems like a minor detail, but just placing yourself in the right position could help you more than you know. Show you care. Show respect. You will receive the same in return.

Where you sit in class is just one example. The point is to identify similar situations where you have control over putting yourself in a situation to succeed. Building good habits will lead to accomplishing big things. It might take some time, but if you start by replacing one bad habit with one good one and continue to build on those, you will be surprised at the result.

Sometimes just making little changes, like where you sit or where you put your shoes in the morning, can trigger your brain to feel different and get you out of a funk. Stick to your principles and dreams, make little changes in your habits, and you will see results. Here are ten examples of other things you can do today to make sure you are taking action in the right direction:

1. Find a notebook. Write things down.
2. Start to self-simulate pressure situations; the more, the better.
3. Replace one bad habit with a good one. Make it routine. Stick with it.
4. Shift your inner voice and the way you talk to yourself. Is it positive? Self-talk is key.
5. Get organized. Make a checklist. Start small.
6. Wake up earlier. Be on your phone less. Time is precious; make it count.
7. Increase discipline; reduce distractions; prioritize time and energy toward your goals.
8. Surround yourself with people going in the same direction.
9. Do a perspective reset. Stop complaining. If you're not happy, do something about it.
10. Be *better* than you were yesterday in a category of your choice. Repeat tomorrow.

4. Discover Your "Chip"

We've probably all heard the phrase, they had a "chip on their shoulder." It usually comes up when an athlete has an increased amount of intensity, focus, and drive. My understanding of the origins of that phrase is that people would put a small chip of wood on their shoulder and dare others to knock it off to evoke a fight.

Belief that you were treated unfairly in the past and that you have something to prove—using whatever example that might be to give yourself an extra source of motivation can be useful. The Ali-and-his-bike example we discussed is one of the most popular, but what made it strong was that it meant a lot to him. Don't dwell on things that have happened to you in the past and that you have no control over, but also don't lose perspective, and it be might something you can use for an extra boost of motivation in a difficult stretch.

5. Train with a Purpose. Do the Extra.

The Iditarod is a sled dog race covering over one thousand miles of some of the most rugged terrain on the planet. The people who are brave enough and win the race are those who know when to follow the blazed trail, but they also know when to wake up in the middle of the night when the others are still sleeping, blaze a new trail, and make the sacrifices needed to set themselves apart!

Key: Everyone gets tired; it is those who are willing to do the extra work and operate even when tired that leave others behind. Those who can operate when they are tired will rule the world. If you are a wrestler, a gymnast, or a lacrosse player, regardless of the sport, this rule applies. The next time you are tired and want to stop, remind yourself that there is someone else out there on a quest to get what you want. You now have a choice. Take a nap and rest, or take advantage of those stopping because they are tired. Don't let others achieve your greatness.

For example, let's say you are in the weight room and you are doing three sets of some type of lift. After the second set, you realize it's too easy, but the heavier weights are all the way on the other side of the weight room. Do you just settle and keep going, or do you go get the heavier ones that you know will make you better? Make the trip across the weight room.

It's Friday, and the coach has just told you to do ten sprints on your own and you can leave for the weekend. You could do eight or nine; no one will ever know. Maybe everyone else does ten. Why not do ten, eleven, or maybe more. This extra time when no one is watching builds up and will set you apart from those just getting by. Show up early and stay late. There are athletes across the world going to practice and doing similar things. That isn't enough. You must train with a purpose, not just show up. How bad do you want it? Stay longer and do the extra, and you will be rewarded. In order to do the extra, you must also do the little things that are expected of you. For example, if you watch a team warm up before a game, there's usually a couple of people not doing the warm-up correctly and just going through the motions. Not stretching correctly is going to lead to injuries and ultimately hurt the team.

You can't do the extra if you can't even do the regular. Do the little things, so you will be asked to do the big things.

Important: Don't worry about what others think. Let your genuine action show your intentions. It's common for young athletes not to want to stay after practice or ask for help because they don't want their teammates to think they are sucking up or a "try hard." Ignore it. Let them be average. If they are really your teammates, they want to see you succeed and care about the team; they will not only hold judgment, but they will also join and do the extra work with you. Imagine if you had a team comprised of athletes all like this; the outcome would be special.

6. Learn What It Means to Listen
Being a good listener takes effort and practice, and it's something the best athletes are willing to do.

It's important to be able to listen to criticism. You don't have to agree, and it might not be warranted, but you should listen. Listening to praise can be equally uncomfortable. The best athletes can learn to accept criticism and pass the praise on to others. You don't learn anything while you are talking. Just listen. If you don't know what to say, don't say anything. Just listen. If you're ever in doubt, don't say anything. It's ok. You don't have to have an opinion about everything.

Tip: Make sure to appreciate who that are willing to genuinely listen to you. When you have the chance to do the same for someone else, they'll remember it.

7. Be Creative...Creatively

> "Only those who attempt the absurd can achieve the impossible."
> —Albert Einstein

What if no one ever tried something new? This could be in training, preparation, drills, mindset, and what you do the rest of your life. Be the trendsetter, keep an open mind to new ideas, and don't be afraid to be creative. Use good judgment when having an open mind and trying new things, but don't fear the risk of trying something different. Find your niche and dominate it.

Disclaimer: When doing things differently, you still have to be on the train. You can go to different cars, go up to the caboose, maybe the engine room, or even go up to the top of the train and walk around...but you have to be on the train. If you're too "off the wall" in your creativity, you're going to be left behind. Ask different questions, think outside the box, but make sure you're still on the train. Just like everything else, use good judgment and ask for help.

8. Ask Questions. Take Notes Along the Way.

One of the best decisions I ever made was to write things down from the beginning of my life as a young athlete. Write things down as you go. Goals, quotes, lessons learned, good ideas, bad ideas, inventions, a speech you may one day give, stories, to-do lists, or draw pictures—you never know when you will need them again, and if you're lucky, you will have a chance to share them with others someday, just as I am doing now. Whether it's on your phone or you are writing it down, the practice of taking the time to reflect is what really matters. I'm not smart enough to know why it matters and how it helps, but writing things down is a healthy practice.

Buy a notebook and take notes. Read books. Listen to speakers. Take new classes. Seek knowledge. Continue to learn throughout your life, and you will be rewarded. The ability to ask questions and a desire to know more about us and our planet are some of the most important things that set us apart as humans. Don't let the millions of years of evolution of our brains go to waste.

9. Develop Social Awareness

"A person can have a great idea, but if that person cannot inspire others to buy into that idea, it doesn't matter."
—Carmine Gallo, *The Storyteller's Secret*

In 2016, Carmine Gallo published a book called *The Storyteller's Secret*. He shares that another thing successful people have in common is their ability to tell stories. Clear. Concise. Passionate. You must be able to tell your story in a way that will inspire others if you want your ideas to succeed.

Different situations will require you to act differently. Being aware of your surroundings, the culture, the people present, the context and adapting accordingly is an important skill. Paul Tough of *How Children Succeed* refers to this as "social agility." You don't have to enter a room as if you were running for mayor, but you do need to have enough skills to show your true character. There is a difference between sucking up and being sincere. Make eye contact, have good body language and a firm handshake, and be yourself. That's all anyone wants. Within thirty seconds, you can get an impression of the type of person you are dealing with; make it count. If you have no idea how to act, it's ok; just be you, watch what others are doing, and pick up on their cues. When having a conversation, you can show respect and interest in what they are saying by asking questions, being an active listener, and being present. Social agility is something you will have to master, and it takes practice.

Tip: Grow out of using filler words such as "like" and "umm" before someone tells you that you should. It hurts your credibility and your message, and while it may not seem like a big deal, it is to some. At some point, you have to speak in a way that people will respect; try to start now.

10. Body Language and Controlling Emotion

Poor body language is a mistake I see made by young athletes. It can have a negative impact on your team, yourself, and your future. The athletes who have mastered good body language are never too high or too low. You can't tell by looking at them if they are having a great game or the worst game of their lives; this is critical. If you're the type of athlete who complains and pouts, that's what people will remember about you. It doesn't matter how good you are or how bad the officials are; neither are excuses, and someone is always watching.

Having poor body language will negatively impact your performance and that of your teammates, as it is a great way to suck energy from others. It can also impact your future. While coaching collegiately and recruiting, I would watch the body language of players as closely as I could. How do they respond to failure? Can they control their emotions? Are they looking the coach in the eye when they are being talked to? Are they a front-runner, or are they a good teammate regardless of what's happening on the field?

It's natural to have emotion, but there *is a difference between playing with emotion and playing emotionally.* The goal isn't to suppress emotion or trick yourself into not feeling it. Pay attention, know how to communicate it, and learn to use it as another way to set yourself apart. Showing emotional discipline is not easy, but you really have no other choice. If you catch yourself having poor body language or losing control, take a deep breath, reset, and move on.

There are varying beliefs on why humans even have emotions, but we know everyone shares this part of the human experience. No one is a robot. It impacts what we do, whether we realize it or not. Trying to ignore how you're feeling isn't healthy, but you're missing out on something the *most successful athletes have learned how to turn into something they can use.* An example would be anger. If you can harness it and not let it control you, you can leverage it.

Here are a few more next-level, system-changing ways of life that I see in elite athletes.

Do More Things that Are "Hard"
What this is can vary, but see if you can challenge yourself to do something hard or even something that you didn't really want to do. It could be a workout; it could also be walking the dog, helping your grandma, or sitting at the dinner table with your parents and telling them about your day. The more you do this, the more it will become a habit, and there will be a lot of good, positive results.

Earn Your Equipment
Equipment can be both important and expensive. A suggestion: tell whoever it is that helps you get that equipment that you'd like to figure out a way to earn it. (Unless you're working a part-time job and buying on your own anyway—good for you!) Why would you do this?

It's probably the right thing and would be considerate to offer, but it also gives you a chance to avoid the feeling of being entitled to anything and head into battle knowing you've earned every step, every bat, and every pair of shoes. My own opinion is that if there are skates that are $50 more than another model that you don't like as much, choose the one you'll feel good playing in.

The Best Athletes Mimic, Then Make
Have you ever noticed how the best athletes mimic other athletes early on? They watch what they do, how they do it, mimic them in the driveway, swing like them at the park, and then mesh those into becoming their own, which other kids will one day mimic. There's more to this than it's just "fun" to mimic the athletes at the top of their game. Mimic those that have gone on in a direction where you want to go, and then make your own way when the time is right.

Learn to Identify and "Leverage" the Controllable

This is a trait all elite athletes have but is difficult to quantify. Athletes that set themselves apart don't worry or complain; they find ways to "leverage the controllable parts" of their lives, good or bad, into making it an advantage others don't have.

The word *controllable* is self-explanatory. It's the stuff you have control over. Leveraging is basically using something to your advantage. There are positives to be found in any predicament you might find yourself in. An injury may give you a chance to see your sport from a new perspective; getting cut from a team may provide you with the fire needed or even a new path; not getting the playing time you think you deserve or agreeing with a coach can test your will and willingness to be a good teammate.

If you have a problem and can do something about it, then you have nothing to worry about. If it's out of your control, then spending time worrying won't do you any good. Look for the positives in any situation; it may be the thing you're most thankful for years from now.

There is too much at stake, too many elements you can't control, for you to have your success rely upon the system that you're in. You're the element that you know, have control over, and will be the one that transfers from one system to the next.

If you develop the right kinds of habitats and find the discipline to keep them, believe in yourself even when others don't, and resist the temptation to follow the pack toward a life of normalcy, a lot of extraordinary results await. Don't let a bad coach, or an overly supportive parent, or a lack of resources be the reason your journey stops short of where you hope to go—you won't regret it.

Prepare *Yourself* for Tryouts

This can be a high-stakes, high-anxiety period of the year that will require following the plan set forth but also doing the extra. This is your responsibility. Control what you can control; don't worry about the rest. These are things that can help make sure you're ready to give yourself the best chances at your tryout, and that's all you can really ask for.

1. **Be in shape. Be healthy.**
   a. If you aren't healthy, you can't even tryout. If it requires rest and inaction, do it.
   b. Do more than what they tell you to be ready to do. Example: You're doing a timed two-mile run; train as if you are going to have to go three to four miles.
2. **Know what the tryout format is.**
   a. It doesn't matter if you disagree with what the tests are; get stronger and do the right things.
   b. If you don't know how to prepare, ask questions. Don't guess.
3. **Train hard, but appropriately.**
   a. If there are tests, find out what they are: timed runs, pull-ups, shuttles, etc.
   b. Mental prep: put yourself in the position while training leading up.
4. **Put yourself in the right position, mentally and physically.**
   a. Have a good attitude, wear the right thing, listen, and don't run to the coach's car and ask if you can carry his bag; just show that you really want a spot by how you act.
   b. Visualize what the day will be like and feel like, and put yourself in a position to succeed.

5. **Make a timeline and plan.**
   a. Plan out when you need to be ready and the steps needed to get there. Don't go for a run the week before and think you're good.
   b. Put in the work; it will pay off.

Do what you can to look forward to this part of the process. It doesn't have to be fun, but the need to make sure you're ready and held accountable can be a good thing. Look at it as a way to showcase your hard work and set yourself apart.

No Athlete Can Avoid Every Rut or Slump. The Greats Know How to Work Through

Everyone finds themselves in a "rut" at some point; this is athletics but also life. You know you must work your way out, but you can't get out by using a shovel. Here are some of the tools that will get you out, not dig you deeper into the rut *you* must get yourself out of.

1. **Pause and zoom out.** Take a drone-level view of your current situation. Sometimes a different perspective will put whatever adversity you're facing into the right context.
2. **Think back and look forward.** Think back to past accomplishments and adversity you've had to overcome; there's no reason you can't do it again. Believe in yourself.
3. **Trust your instincts.** This can be hard when times are tough, but your body and your mind often know what they need and will try to tell you. When in doubt, keep moving forward.
4. **Remind yourself that all things change.** Nothing lasts forever, good things or bad things. Whatever adversity you're facing, it will pass.

5. **Work through it.** What this means will vary from athlete to athlete, but sometimes it can be working out, going for a run, or taking extra reps, but doing nothing won't help.

Tip: It's not possible, nor the goal, to never be in a slump or feel like you're in a rut. The goal really is to shorten the duration, know how to avoid it and if and when you do find yourself there, be able to learn from it and move on.

Some Common Mistakes Athletes Make and Should Avoid

1. **Too tentative;** Sometimes when you want something so badly, you can become tentative. Don't be afraid to fail or make a mistake, and don't worry what your stats may be at the end of the day. It is possible that you could fail, but will you ever be able to forgive yourself if you don't try? Another mistake athletes will often make here is waiting for things to be absolutely perfect, the right time to ask, the right time to start doing more—don't wait. Go for it.
2. **Overreact or underappreciate:** "I made an error; it is the end of the world." No it's not, learn from it, show your resilience, and move forward. The other mistake here is that athletes often don't appreciate all the great things until it is too late. Take some time to look around and appreciate what you have even when times are tough.
3. **Distractions impacting destiny**
    a. **Relationships:** Give your time and energy to those who appreciate it. Don't let a bad relationship with

friends or significant others keep you from reaching your goals. Form alliances with people with the same trajectory.
  b. **Parties:** Be smart. One party isn't worth getting all that you worked so hard for taken away. There will always be more parties.
  c. **Worrying about what others think:** Don't get caught up in worrying about what others think of petty things like your clothes, pictures, or posts. Anyone worth caring about wouldn't care about these things.
  d. **Handling prosperity:** It is sometimes harder to handle prosperity than adversity. Fewer people may be willing to help you, can bring comfort, distract from your routine, and remove the inspiration of being an underdog. Find new ways to motivate yourself, and don't let some success prevent more of it.
  e. **Technology:** Our phones and other forms of technology are designed to suck us into hours of mindless scrolling. Don't let this be you.
4. **The curse of comparison:** Comparing ourselves to others isn't something new to athletes, but social media has put comparison on steroids. Comparing ourselves to others, without any context, can be a mistake and a curse athletes need to avoid.
5. **The blamer:** "It's not my fault." When you mess up, don't let your mom convince you that it was someone else's fault or that you are owed something without earning it. Take responsibility. Be accountable. And make sure your drive and decisions match what you say your dreams are. It's common for athletes to say they really want it but aren't really willing to do what it takes.

6. **Stat stalker:** Don't let stats ruin your experience. If you work hard, good things will happen. "You get what you put in; people get what they deserve." Worrying about your stats is only going to make it harder on you to perform at a high level. Focus on the process; don't worry about things you have no control over, and the stats will follow.
7. **Tweet, text, turmoil:** Once you post, tweet, or text something, there is no taking it back. Be careful about posting anything, especially prematurely. It's not worth having those regrets.
8. **Quit due to a coach:** It's common for athletes to say, "Oh yeah, I quit because I didn't like the coach." There might be coaches who you don't agree with, or maybe you feel you didn't get a fair shake. Don't let that be the reason you quit being an athlete. Learn from it, move forward, and don't let an adult rob you of the magic of being a young athlete and the skills that can come from it.
9. **"No one told me to":** It is a mistake to think that someone will always be there to push you. Don't wait for someone to tell you to do the extra to make you work hard. Take it upon yourself to get motivated, and be disciplined enough to keep it.
10. **Caring about the can't controls:** This is an easy trap to fall into, hard to avoid, but important to remember. It's common for athletes to spend too much time, any time, worrying about things they can't control or worrying about what "might" happen.

Tip: Don't worry about doing all of these things, all at once, all the time moving forward; no one is perfect, and that's not the goal. But remember that any improvement is an improvement.

Know When to Recalibrate: Stoking the Fire

If you've ever been camping and started a fire, you know every fire requires the same basic ingredients: oxygen, fuel (ex. wood), and heat. Over time, even the best, well-designed, and most adequately fueled fires need to be stoked: the act of poking, prodding, or adding more fuel. As the wood settles, the fuel becomes too spread out, there's really not a lot of oxygen flow, but with just a few well-placed pokes, the flame will reignite. It wasn't reignited by dumping a ton of gas on it or giving a swift kick; it was done by someone who knows the fire and what it needed. If it's your own fire you're trying to reignite, think back to what it was that started that fire in the first place. You will know best what you need and how much of it. In most cases, it's not a matter of adding to the fire but *repositioning what's already inside.* It's not the first hot flame that the success of a fire is determined by, but the long burning logs you can get to stay warm long into the night after you are gone.

Most will say they want it. Many will start. Few are willing to do what it takes to get it. If you want to be the best version of yourself in athletics and beyond, these skills are important. Show others that character and integrity are important to you on your quest to set yourself apart as an athlete. If you want to exceed all expectations, you will need help from others on your journey. Think about where you want to go, the steps it will take to get there…and get going.

7

UNDERSTANDING AND UTILIZING AN IMPORTANT ALLY—THE ADULTS

This book is an example of the impact an adult can have on an athlete. If you can understand and utilize this resource, it will help you reach your goals and could impact the rest of your life.

It's not easy being an adult in the world of a young athlete. It is a different kind of challenge than what you're facing, but the purpose of this chapter is to give some perspective on the role of the adults you may encounter along the way and how to leverage and navigate this complicated but critical section of life together. You can't get to the top of this mountain alone. Adults can help you get there, but you also need to do what you can to protect yourself from an adult being the reason you end your story as an athlete. The adults aren't going anywhere. This is *your* journey.

The obvious adults we think of here are parents and coaches, but there are adults we'll cross paths with on the periphery of athletics that are extremely important, sometimes more so than the ones teaching us anything sports related. Teachers, for example, play a key role in that they can give you the support needed but also a safe environment that gives you a chance to get mentorship and guidance without the pressure of it being connected to the sport you're passionate about.

(Note: You're going to be an adult yourself someday (or are already). Putting yourself in other people's shoes is going to give you a better perspective on what it means to be them and what challenges they face, but this will also improve your perspective on what it means to be an athlete now.)

If you're thinking right now, *No one has a worse parent situation than me*. Maybe they do way too much and are in your face constantly, or they don't care and have never come to a game, or they are going through things that have nothing to do with sports or you. The key is understanding and utilizing a resource that you have no choice but to need, navigate, and maybe even nurture in your life along the way. Finding a mentor(s) who believes in you before you do and can help you become the person you aspire to be. This can be a life-changing connection that can't be replicated.

Identify the Adult who Wants the Best for You as a Human, Not Just as an Athlete

This is complicated and isn't my place to tell you whether how an adult is treating you is good for you or misplaced, but it's important that you know the difference and that both exist. A club coach can have the incentive of getting paid to coach you, but they also wants to see you do well. A parent may yell at you all the time, never say a word about your sport, or come to a single game, and both care the same amount. Remember, unless you're the youngest of five, this is all new to your parents, and they're trying to figure it out too.

If you feel as if the adult genuinely cares about what happens to you outside of your season—which includes what kind of grades you're getting, how you're treating others, and if you're both challenged and happy—this is a good indicator and someone you should feel good about taking advice from. And if you do feel like they're just in it for themselves, the money, or living vicariously through you to relive their days as an athlete, you've got to figure out a way to advocate for yourself, and don't be afraid to ask for help. If it feels off, you're probably right.

A mistake I see athletes make here is that they try to make these assessments on their own. Giving someone who berates you the benefit of the doubt that they are just hard on you because they care sometimes isn't warranted. It could be that they're just not good communicators, but you should get other people's perspectives. We sometimes have blinders in terms of those close to us, and we shouldn't be quick to judge, but that goes with trust too.

> **"Define the goals, put roles and communication methods in place, define the path to the goal, and meet in the middle at the desired destination."**
> —Kate Leavell

Coach/Athlete Sliding Spectrum

The following illustration represents the importance of the sliding spectrum between athlete and coach. Both are responsible for "adjusting" and being flexible to meet the other in the middle. The best coaches and teachers can read and adapt, same goes for athletes. Neither entity should have to give in on principles or be someone they are not, but rather they should adjust to meet needs and help reach potential.

Note: Coaches don't want athletes who don't listen to them, just as athletes do not coaches who don't listen. Coaches also don't want athletes who will only do what they tell them and nothing more. What does that mean? The best athletes know when to make decisions that they know they need to make and when to listen. Depending on the coach and the situation, you may need to meet them in the middle and be flexible. Ask questions that will help you get better and be the kind of athlete you would want to coach. Everyone wins.

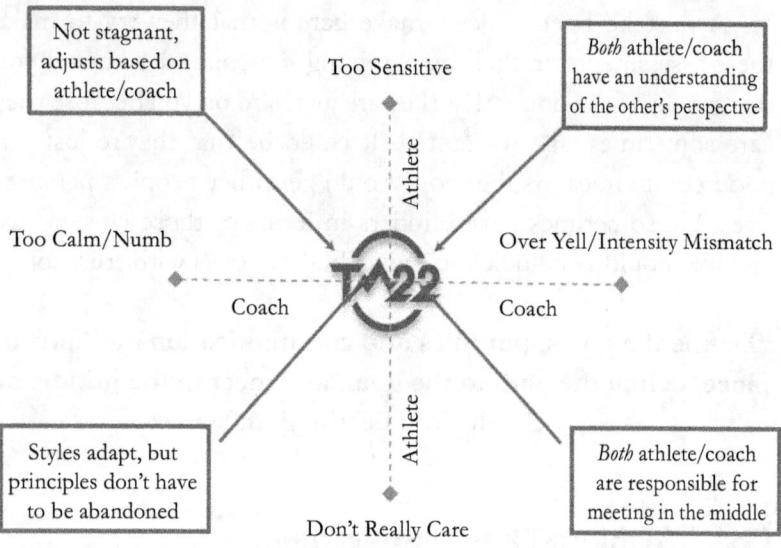

Athletes and coaches both want discipline, and both must work to meet the other on the spectrum. Sometimes one part of this equation may need to adjust more than the other to make it work. There are non-negotiables coaches should have (e.g., effort);

the other values can be determined by the team and unleash the power of player-driven expectations.

Be Open Minded and Willing to Adapt to Different Coaching Styles

The best athletes can learn something from even the worst coaches. Throughout your career as an athlete, you are going to have coaches with a variety of styles, including some great coaches and probably also less than great coaches. Don't let them impact your destiny on this mountain. Adapt to different styles, such as not taking it personally if your coach is a yeller or taking advantage of a coach that never says anything. Adapt, learn to be coachable under different styles, and be glad if a coach says anything to you. Hopefully it means they care, they know you are willing to be coached, and it may be the only style they know.

Embrace Parent and Coach "Craziness"

Most parents will admit they can go a little bit (or entirely) crazy or behave out of character during this time in your life. Embrace those times your mom is acting like a lunatic, your dad is telling you "good job" after going 0–15 shooting, and your grandparents rang a cowbell for three straight hours at your gymnastics meet. There are kids who don't have any parents to come to their games or sometimes even come home. It's hard to be a parent. It's not an excuse. Just remember they've also embarked on a hard, unpredictable journey, and they probably care more about what happens to you than themselves. There is no family transfer portal. If something bothers you, let your parents know. Tell them how they can help. And when your mom says, "Good job, honey," after playing the worst game of your life, just smile and say thanks. She just wants you to be happy and may not know what else to say. And that's ok.

Standing Up to the Parents in the Stands

I love sports. I love watching sports. Being in the stands at a youth sporting event may be my least favorite place to be on the planet. It's embarrassing. You can't help but cringe. We all can picture it. Most will agree, parents included, that people lose their minds and become possessed by irrational comments and "support." Being a stubborn adult is one thing, but yelling at another person's kid, a teenager, or retired vet who is volunteering to officiate is just not ok. My best advice here is to know everyone deals with it. Try to laugh about it. If it's your parent, do your best to explain that them that yelling "focus" or "*shoot*" when the coach has a play written up for you to pass is just making things worse. *You don't need them to yell to know that they care.* When it's your turn to be in the stands someday, play a part in putting a stop to continuing this unfortunate tradition of youth sports.

Tip: Break the cycle: It's common that when we see parents doing something, yelling at the refs, coaching from the stands, or yelling at you in the car on the way home, it's probably because that's what their parents did to them. Their thinking is that if they survived it, they are what they are today, and they need to do that for you too. You know better than anyone right now what it feels like, and it's often just a bad copy. There's a difference between continuing their principles and trying to replicate teaching styles. You can help, support, and show you care without losing control and berating kids from another team, coach, or official. Break the cycle.

Be Coachable and Assume Good Intentions

Show up on time, pay attention, listen, and be open to new ideas. If you can do these things, you will benefit and become the best athlete possible. Even if you don't agree or have heard it before, being coachable means that coaches will continue to want to work with you and will care about what happens to you. If you aren't coachable, you are going to have a hard time finding people willing to help you. One coach doesn't take any one athlete from the base to the summit; it's a relay, held together by a common core. It's the coach's job to teach the athlete skills and get them ready for the next phase. It's your job as the athlete to get what you can, when you can, and keep adding those skills and experiences to your quiver.

Building a Well-Rounded, Max-Potential Athlete Is a Team Effort

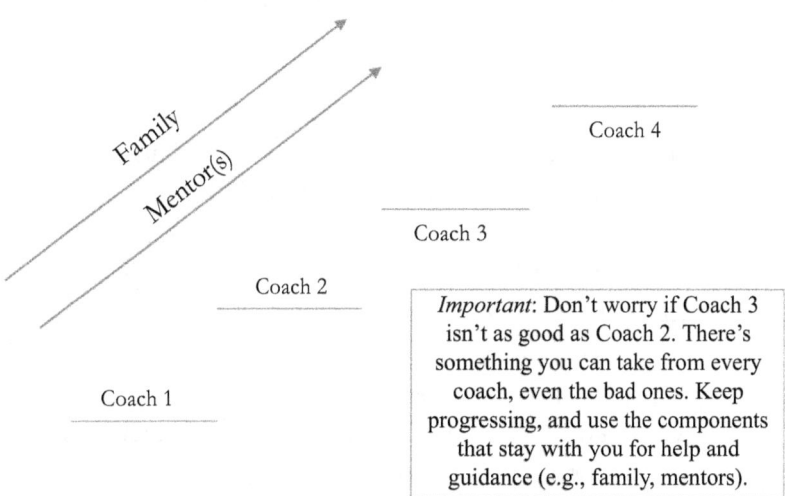

Important: Don't worry if Coach 3 isn't as good as Coach 2. There's something you can take from every coach, even the bad ones. Keep progressing, and use the components that stay with you for help and guidance (e.g., family, mentors).

Improve Your Ability to Assess the Quality of Advice and Who to Trust

Along the way, you're going to have to make countless decisions. Decisions such as what to eat, who to hang out with, and how to spend your time—these are small but can add up. Bigger decisions will follow and include things like deciding which college to attend.

Lots of people are going to be giving you advice, whether you ask for it or not, so how do you know if the advice you're getting is good? And should you even trust that person and their intentions?

Indicators of Good Advice

This is something that you just don't know yet at a young age, and you'll have figured it out when you're older. Adults are constantly navigating this too. It's hard. Start to learn now what the indicators are and how you can help navigate the advice being sent your way.

Here are a few categories that may help identify good advice you can use:

1. **Trust your gut.** You have instincts and intuition inside of you. No one knows you better than you, and sometimes you just have to make decisions based on the information you have at the time. Tip: Don't let making a decision freeze you. Not every decision is going to be perfect, and there are going to be mistakes along the way, but if you do what "feels right," that decision is going to sit better with you and give you the best chance of making the right ones.
2. **Understand the source and diversify.** Sometimes what can happen if you just ask advice from the same person or the same department or group of people is that you will get a very narrow type of advice. Example: Everyone from the English department says you are a talented poet and should pursue that path. They see and know this side of you, but they are probably motivated to encourage you on a path that they know. This isn't always bad; understand that people will have bias, and you should get advice from different sources, not just one coach, teacher, or parent. If

you hear it from multiple sources, it's probably good advice. Look for those that have what you want and that is usually the best source of good advice for that path.
3. **Be open minded and listen.** But don't forget about your principles and what makes you you. (Oh, this is what I did, and it worked, so you should too.) Are they saying that because it will make them feel better about a decision they made in their own lives? Remember, this is your path, your journey. Good advice will feel as if it's helping you beyond just one skill in one season, and it may be something you weren't expecting to hear. Have an open mind, but know that ultimately you should be the one making decisions that will impact your own self-interest.

Learn *Who* to Trust

If you've ever had the feeling of having your trust broken, you know how hard it is to put your trust back in that person or even others. You shouldn't just give your trust away freely, but ultimately, putting your trust in others, when appropriate, is a tool that can help set you apart. Here are a few sources who can typically be relied upon to give you advice that's best for you.

Tip: Have these discussions with your parents, especially when talking about identifying the other adults you encounter to trust and what their motivation to help you might be.

1. **Your parents:** You should trust, or at least hope, that your parents have your best interests in mind. This doesn't mean they're perfect or don't make mistakes, but most parents want their kids to succeed. What you need to identify is what the definition of success is to them. It could be different than yours.

2. **The adult that you know *is in your corner*:** If it's clear to you that an adult cares about what happens to you beyond your one season with them as your coach or beyond the sport that you play, that's a good indicator that they're willing to tell you the truth and give you advice that doesn't mask an ulterior motive. Being in your corner is meant to define the adult that, regardless of how you perform, you know will be there and won't give up on you. Sometimes these adults aren't the ones you'd expect.
3. **Yourself:** Again, being an athlete can cause you to constantly question yourself, and you'll be tempted to give up, cave in, or listen to someone who is saying you can't. Don't let that happen. No one knows you better than you, and there just isn't an alternative here. If you don't trust yourself, no one will.

Big Decisions that Matter: Choosing a College and the Adults to Trust

There is no shortage of videos and tools online to help you improve your fundamentals. Your own self-discipline and motivation will be critical in setting yourself apart. But when it comes to making a decision about what to do after high school and what for most is the biggest decision of their lives, you'll need more than a video or instinct. Adults can help you, but it's important to look closely at what their motivations might be. It's common that the advice you'll get is "what they chose." That doesn't make it right or what's right for you.

I saw this mark on a concrete sidewalk one day while walking home. I don't remember the context, but I remember feeling sorry for myself and seeing this and thinking, "There's always a choice,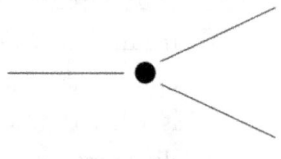

about what to do, how to react, what to do next." Some decisions have bigger impacts than others and could create a whole other set of choices. (The mark on the concrete was from a masonry-surveying tool.)

The Young Athlete Years	**Post-College/Professional Career**
Life is a network of decisions, all connected, some bigger than others. In the beginning, the choices may seem small, but they determine the next steps to follow. Use these to gain experience and perspective.	After college, the decisions don't stop, but now most of them will be done on your own, making decisions that impact others and in a position where you'll be helping others make decisions of their own.

Choosing the sport(s) you want to play and who your friends are are examples of early decisions that send you down a certain path.

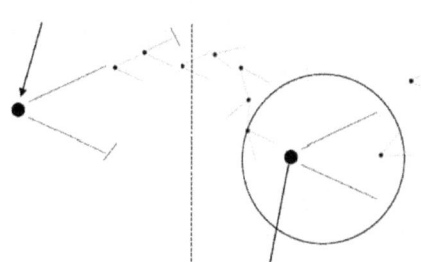

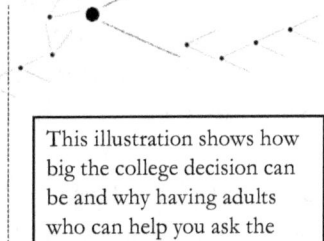

This illustration shows how big the college decision can be and why having adults who can help you ask the right questions is key.

Choosing a college or post-high school path is the biggest decision most will make at this point in their lives. You've got to figure out how to make the best decision for your current and future post-athlete future selves.

> **Some Advice:** Don't get stuck on looking for what you envision is the "ideal situation"—the perfect coach, the perfect opportunity to play, the perfect distance from your friends. "Perfect" doesn't exist, and if it does, getting exactly what you think you need may not be ideal.

How to Make the "Right" Choice and What That Feels Like

There are a myriad of variables that are unique to you—your sport, your family. It's impossible for me, this book, or any other to tell you what factors you should consider. It's just got to "feel right." Note: Be careful not to confuse what feels right with what feels comfortable.

Let's be clear: the goal here is to find a situation that is the right fit for you and your family. If you're fortunate enough to have more than one choice (or any choice at all), you're going to have to face the reality that there will be a path you'll never know what it would have led to and be ok with the choice you make. You can avoid having any regrets by doing your research, doing what you think is best for you and not because of a significant other or to be with friends you're comfortable with. It's hard to explain, but some places just "feel" better than others. Trust your instincts here on what fit feels best, and you won't regret it.

Advice: If you're faced with options you didn't think you'd have or were hoping for something else, sometimes not getting what you think you want turns out to be the best. Whatever path you choose, it's up to you to make it what you want it to be. Adults can help you make this important decision. *Listen to those who are helping you figure out the right questions, not the ones eager to give you answers they think you want to hear.*

Umpires/Officials and Their Role on the Young-Athlete Team

Umpires, referees, and officials play a role on this path too. There is no doubt—below-average officiating of a game can be frustrating. It can be even more frustrating when the officials themselves seem as if they don't care, have an ego, or just simply aren't doing the best they can. I choose to believe that 99 percent of those who take this position are trying to do their best. I have been a coach for many years and can think of examples of umpires that either had no business being there or were doing it for the wrong reasons, but I can also think of some great ones. Let me focus on what made one umpire so great, and it wasn't his calls.

Charlie Fuller, a long-time resident of Owatonna, Minnesota, was the umpire for the majority of our home games while playing baseball in Waseca. It was always a one-man show; he never had another umpire on the bases or in the outfield, and of course, there was no instant-replay system. I can remember some calls that I thought he didn't get right, and I can remember the dugout giving him a hard time on more than one occasion. But what I remember more is how he treated the players; he had a smile on his face when he arrived at the park and would always say hello. While there was a chance that he might miss a call from time to time, there was never a doubt that he was there to do his best, keep the kids safe, and do his part in creating a fair game environment. He always did his best, just like we ask of our players. That's all we can ask.

On June 4, 2016, he passed away at the age of seventy-six. It wasn't until I read his obituary that I learned about all the amazing things he accomplished in his community, for baseball in Owatonna, his family, and the positive impact he had on the lives of so many young athletes. He was one of us. It was a reminder to me that we're all going through something; if he wasn't willing to come and give his time to a bunch of kids in a neighboring town, there was no game.

The next time you find yourself verbally attacking an umpire for a questionable call, remember that you may not know the whole story and assume they are trying their best. Bad calls are part of the game. The best example you can set for your teammates, your coach, and even your parents is to take the high road and show them that you can't let it bother you.

One solution may be that instead of separating ourselves as much as we can from them and treating them like enemies, we include them more. Invite them to practice so they can work on their calls and your players can get to know them outside of the game atmosphere; maybe let the players try to officiate alongside them to see how hard it is. This also creates the opportunity to have conversations about what calls are the most difficult for them; the players can share what is frustrating to them; and mutual respect can only help. Anyone who has ever officiated a game knows how hard it is and how it feels when people unfairly criticize judgment calls. These adults have an important job in creating a safe, fair environment for our athletes, and it's important we understand their needs as well and include them in our team moving forward.

Why Having the *Right People* Involved Matters

If you really care about something, surround it with good people. That doesn't mean perfect or experts, just good people who care. Little things will never become big things, and whether it's a project, a family, a business, or a youth soccer league, the humans will make all the difference.

In our current youth sports environment, coaches and officials are getting berated, with diminishing amounts of support and reassurance from athletic directors and administrators. We are seeing a decline in those agreeing to be officials or coaches, even when their own kids are involved. As the pool of willing adults gets smaller, it makes finding the right adults to help even harder. If we get to a point where we don't have enough coaches or officials, there will be no sports, or there will be sports filled with those that are there for the wrong reasons. Money, self-fulfillment, and ego—these are not good motivators. The games won't be fair; they won't be fun for you or anyone; they just won't be worth it for families.

Some of my best years as a young athlete had the fewest wins, but the coaches were good people, they cared, and I'm still benefiting from them twenty-five years later. That's the goal. As an athlete, you can impact the number and types of adults wanting to help current and future athletes.

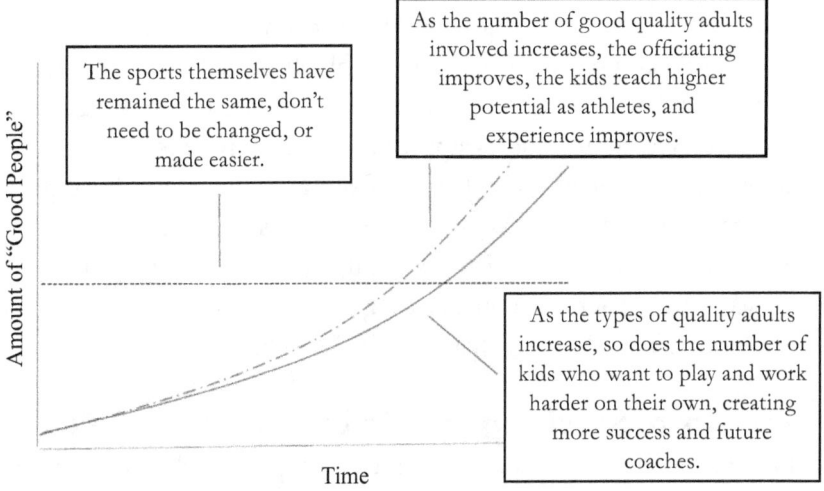

What Can You (the Athlete) Do to Entice the Right Kinds of People to Want to Help?

The player-coach relationship in sports is a conduit of mentorship that can't be replicated. Over time, the philosophy/coaching strategies may change, but never the need for good people. Let's clarify that *good* doesn't mean they need to have doctorates in sports psychology or be a D1 coach or hold records at their high school. The people we want are those who genuinely care about the whole athlete and aren't afraid to push them to help them reach their potential.

Tip: Don't seek out coaches and teachers that get described as "so cruise" or "so chill." This doesn't help you, and while it is tempting to have someone just let you and your friends do what you want, it's a waste of your time, and they're not the kind of adult that's really doing what they can to help you get where you want to go. It's an easy trap to fall into, and most do.

People like being asked for advice and are willing to give it if you're willing to listen, show an effort to improve and put in the work, and can hold yourself accountable. It doesn't have anything to do with being perfect or results. If an adult trusts that you are trying to get better and is appreciative of their perspective and advice, it can be a win-win. It is critical that we maintain this intergenerational connector. With it becoming easier and easier to find whatever information you want within seconds, the information, advice, and impact that comes with getting it from a mentor/coach is a lot different than a website or AI smart ball.

The Art of Surviving and Embracing the Car Ride

Picture the scenario where you put two people together, trap them in a small environment, and force them to be with each other after both have gone through hours of high anxiety, pressure, and elements of failure in front of other people. Both are hungry, and both have homework, work, and dinner to make to ensure the survival of the humans they are responsible for. It sounds like a torture situation. It's almost comical how miserable (for all) this can be. This is the car ride home from a game/practice most athletes and their families go through multiple times a week.

This car ride home from a practice/game can be a period of time that can drive families apart, end the desire to play sports altogether for some, and has the ability to make every passenger miserable, whether they were involved or not. There are some unique challenges that the close confines of a vehicle and the timing of this event seem to escalate.

To start, being able to accept criticism and listen, even when it's not easy, is important. Don't instantly go to your phone. Give yourself some time to dial down, embrace the pain, and then move on. If there are actions you can take to prevent from feeling that way, make a note in your phone or write it down and follow through. It's hard, but it's important. Think of it as strength training for your brain and toughness, if you move away from it as soon as it feels uncomfortable you've lost the growth opportunity. If someone is talking to you, you should listen. That has nothing to do with sports; it's showing respect. Even if you disagree with what they are saying, there is no excuse not to listen when someone is talking to you. Parents are trying to help, which doesn't mean they're right, but you might have to take a deep breath and listen. You're the most important thing to them; they just have no idea what to say but feel like they have to say something.

Note: It's hard to be a parent—period—but especially when they see you unhappy. Sports will do that. They've been at work all day, have a boss they don't like, and may be paying a lot of money for you and your siblings to play sports, and this feels like the one thing they have control of all day.

A huge regret I have is feeling sorry for myself coming home from games (which was usual even if I went 4–5). I'd dwell on the one time I didn't succeed. I'm embarrassed by it. I wasn't mature enough to see how negatively that was impacting those around me. It was selfish on my part. It wasn't intentional. One of the fondest memories I have as an athlete and will always treasure is driving to Windom, Minnesota, with my dad in 1995 for a hockey tournament. Whenever I hear the song Hotel California by the Eagles, I get transported back in time to what that drive felt like, the smell of the arena, and just a positive memory of time spent with my dad. You never know what experiences will stick and what you will regret if you don't do your part in making them positive.

Increase Your "Negative-Adult-Impact Immunity"

Increasing our "immunization levels" is something we're all too familiar with following 2020. Being an athlete requires you to put in so much time, so much energy, and so much sacrifice, but you can't let others rob you of the true gold that comes from being a young athlete. The good news is there are ways you can "increase your immunity" to adults who aren't helping you but hurting your quest.

It seems as if it's becoming more and more common for an athlete to quit due to reasons outside of their own choosing. Not liking a coach, parents trying to overhelp or not at all, or misinterpreting why it is that someone wants you to play a sport can get confusing. You shouldn't feel forced to play, but it should be determined by you for the right reasons, or you'll regret it. If at some point after you read this and want to stop playing, it doesn't make you a failure or a quitter. There are lots of reasons to switch directions and follow your passion, which is what this book would encourage. Just make sure it's for a reason you can live with and on your terms, not someone else's. A few examples:

"I quit because I didn't like my coach."
This isn't going to sit well with you one day. We've all had bad coaches. Unless your safety is in jeopardy, grind through it, learn what you can, and don't let it be what stops your journey.

"I wasn't getting any playing time."
Advocate for yourself. Coaches want athletes to talk to them directly first, before you have your parents reach out. Tell your parents you're going to do this, and practice what you'll say and how you'll say it. I know that the answer might just be that there is someone better than you and/or there just aren't enough spots. At least you'll know, and you'll feel better about asking.

"My club coach doesn't care; they're just here to win games and get paid."
This is entirely possible. It's part of the deal with club sports. Don't take it personally, and it doesn't mean you can't learn from them. Understand what their motivation is, and it is possible that they are doing it because parents are willing to pay them, *and* they want to pay it forward genuinely.

"My dad just wants me to play because he did, and he was really good."
This is common; a parent wants their kid to have the same experiences and joys, and learn the same amount of important skills that they did. It can get blurred sometimes when parents are trying to recreate what they had and how they felt about it, and when it's not the same, it seems like no one is happy. The hope here is that the parent will understand, over time, that this has to be your journey. You can meet in the middle by trying to take their advice and listening. They feel fortunate that they have something they can share with you.

"My mom posts a million pictures of me on social media."
This isn't something anyone can claim they know what it feels like until they have it, but they're proud. If it bothers you, be honest

and say something about it. Maybe there are other ways they can be proud of you and show their friends you're doing well, but they also protects your privacy.

Being an athlete (and in life) is not about getting everything you want all the time. I worry more about the athlete who has gotten everything they've asked for. This is going to show when toughness is needed the most, maybe during the season but definitely later in life. I'm not convinced that even if you could handpick every adult around you your whole life, you'd want that. It's going to rob you of what makes sports so great and worth all the time, sweat, and tears.

Don't let your parents write college coaches emails; that's your job. Don't let others make excuses for you, be accountable, and accept the good and the bad. And try to put yourself in the shoes of the adults from time to time. The adults are making sacrifices you'll never know about. This could be working more to afford lessons, putting up with a boss they don't get respect from but need to support your family, shelving their own passions, hobbies, etc. for *your* goals. This shouldn't add more pressure; just know it exists, and someday you can pay it forward. Sometimes the hardest thing is to not get you or tell you what you want. They know you need it.

Don't ask the adults on your path for easy excuses, but for encouragement and a fair environment that allow you to get the full athlete experience, good and bad. Parents are good at making you do the things you just really don't want to do, but you know you have to. Elite athletes can identify and act on things that they don't want to do but do them without having to be told. I want to share an example of an illustration showing how I think the adults are missing the mark in their (our) attempts to help and the important role you (athletes) really play here.

22—A GUIDE FOR YOUNG ATHLETES

Committing All Resources to Educating Parents/Coaches

Should this be part of the solution? Of course, but it's only one part. Athletes aren't included as much as they should be, and we keep providing resources and conferences for the same group of parents that are already seeking improvement, agree, and can afford. We need a diverse group of adults at the table, and athletes, and make sure those that really need it are represented.

Taking the Sport out of Sport

It's not the sport's fault. The goals aren't too small, competition isn't too hard, too many rules, not enough trophies, or playing time is too hard to earn. It's what makes sports great; if we change the game, it will dilute the outcomes that make this path so important.

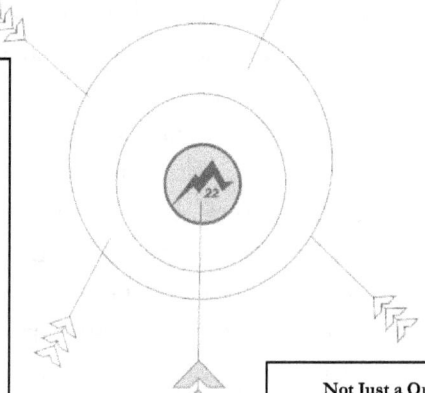

Over-Support, Constant Presence, Underachievement

You could argue helping too much is worse than no help. Unneeded pressure, robbing athletes of important lessons and growth, stealing joy of having their own journey is a common result.

There needs to be struggle for growth. Being at every practice to "support" your athlete isn't helping that athlete more; there needs to be amounts of failure to create the room for success.

The Golden Arrow?

The solution that will produce authentic, sustained change and improvement and equip and empower our athletes. Why?

- This is their path, their journey, not ours. We (adults) can help create the environment, but the athlete should be allowed to earn it and grow.

- If we spend time and resources helping our athletes learn skills that can help overcome adversity, how to find enjoyment in doing things that are challenging, and the true value in having character and being a good teammate, regardless of coach, parent, or ref, the athlete can succeed.

(Golden Arrow does not imply the only option, but a key component.)

Not Just a Quest for Fun

I think we're confusing the words *fun* and *enjoyment*. Sometimes swimming lap after lap after lap isn't really "fun," but the best athletes enjoy the feeling of accomplishment and earning improvement.

If you sign up for sports to seek fun as an intermediate athlete, it's not going to match expectations.

Coaches are not there to entertain your child. It's part of the athlete's responsibility to make it fun, find fulfillment in things that are hard, and feel good about having to earn it. There are a lot of things families can choose to do that are fun and bring joy to their children and family. Sports are fun, but if it's the only reason you're playing or expect someone to make them fun for you, you might be disappointed.

Important: Elite athletes don't want easy or excuses; they just want encouragement and the environment to earn it. When some of the first young athletes were learning tracking skills from their elders around a campfire a long time ago, they were given components, knowledge, and encouragement, but they were also empowered to teach themselves. The elders knew this was the best way to teach if they wanted what was best for their future. Those young humans were forced to analyze the information given to them, think critically about how to apply it, and then make the right decision. That still applies today. Think of the adults around you as members of your team; each has their strengths/weaknesses, and no one has the answers to everything. Figure out a way to work together, and if you have an adult, or several, be grateful that even if they're not perfect, they want what's best for you. They're an important ally on your journey. Do your best to understand and utilize this resource.

Before we move on to looking at more models and tools that can help set us apart, take a moment to think about all those hours we're asking the adults to spend in a cold ice arena, sit in traffic, spend money for a showcase across the United States, and the emotional toll it can take on a house. This is a level of maturity I never had when I was a young athlete and regret it. Find a sincere way to show your gratitude for the sacrifices being made on your behalf.

Remember, the adults may not be sure what their life is going to look like after *your* journey as a young athlete is over. Everyone is going through something, even the most "rock-steady parent."

> **"Getting the right people in the right roles in support of your goal is the key to succeeding at whatever you choose to accomplish."**
> —Ray Dalio, *Principles*

8

THE YOUNG ATHLETE DEN—MODELS, FORMULAS, AND TOOLS

The journey of athletes and what it takes to be successful continues to evolve; so should we.

Movies that include adventure and long journeys will often have the characters find (or stumble upon) a cave with mysterious petroglyphs, a room in a castle with tables full of books and maps, or a laboratory with equations and data from past experiments. Regardless of the space, you can clearly see people have been spending a lot of time thinking, creating, and trying to solve a problem(s). Imagine that in our case that room had information that you knew could help you be a better athlete and reach your potential. This is the "athlete den" and is the intent of this chapter.

Definitions of a "den" can include: a place to study, work, relax, and think, the shelter of a wild animal; even a hide out for outlaws. Here it's a place for athletes to gain perspective and look at models to help you think, understand, and apply to your own quest.

Note: When I read books, I appreciate when the authors attempt to illustrate what they're trying to understand and offer some of type of tool to address it. The goal isn't to make the reader accept or agree with them, but it helps offer a new way of thinking about it. This is that part of the book. (To increase the effectiveness of this chapter, consider having your parents read it. You may need help putting these tools into action, and asking their advice will benefit you.)

Explanation of Den Format

Each of the problems, challenges, and opportunities chosen in this chapter are complex and could probably have a chapter (or book) of their own, but that model wouldn't allow you to have the information you need in the window when you really need it. It's not a shortcut; we're just attempting to streamline the information and provide a path for the information to be usable. Below is an example of these types of models and attempts to illustrate why timing is key.

The Peak Window: Align Experience and Knowledge with Timing and Opportunity

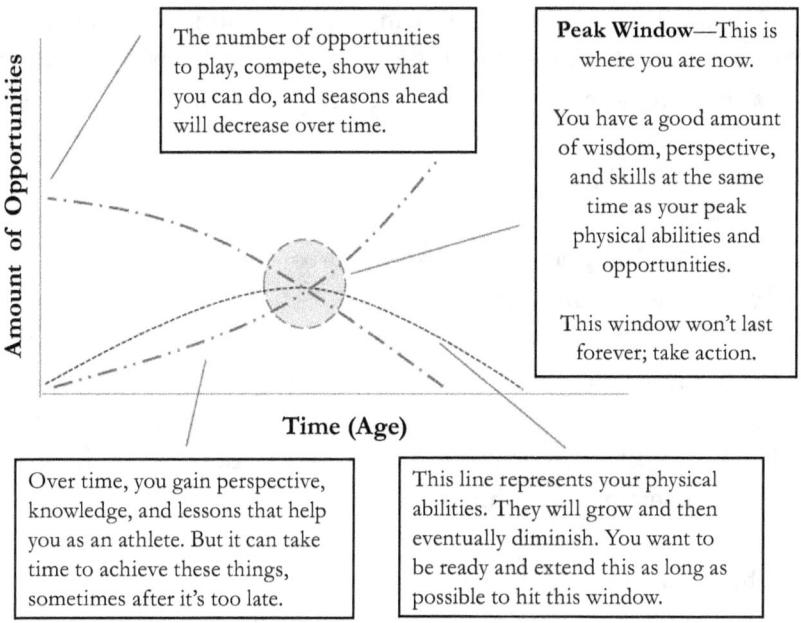

Tip: Remember, it's never too late to start or adjust your trajectory. You don't need permission.

The challenges targeted in this chapter are complex, but with the challenge comes opportunity. For more models and discussion, visit tm22athletes.com. Here are the five challenges targeted in this chapter:

1. Designing the elite-athlete formula and foundation
2. Creating your own compass, checkpoints, and coordinates
3. Taking time and building balance

4. Protecting and promoting yourself as an athlete
5. Managing anxiety—pregame, during game, and life

(Are there more challenges than this? Of course, but these are important in building the proper foundation and navigating what has become some of the more complex parts of being an athlete.)

Bonus: A Tool to Help Move Forward

Model 1: Designing the Elite-Athlete Formula and Foundation

The Challenge/Opportunity: It's critical that athletes have the right components, are properly balanced, and are built upon the proper foundation. So what are they, and what does that look like? Look carefully at the components, and see if your current life as an athlete contains these things.

The Critical Components

You must have the right ingredients or the recipe and cook really don't matter. The situation you are in is different, but these are important components regardless of external variables. These core components should be present year-round and take precedence over supplemental components. It's possible your core components may differ, and that's ok; just make sure that these components remain untouched and are what you're fighting to protect.

List of Supplemental Components

The supplemental components cover a wide spectrum of on-and-off-the-field areas important to creating an effectively balanced, healthy, happy, and excelling athlete. Every athlete is different, and there are additional components unique to every situation. Adjust as needed.

- **Build the Dream**
  - Remember that creating a vision that motivates us is key. Take time to watch; observe athletes playing at a level you someday wish to be at. Learning about people pursuing their dreams off the field can be valuable as well.
- **Expand the Comfort Zone**
  - You must learn to get comfortable with being uncomfortable. Pushing yourself on and off the field is important if you wish to improve. Seek ways on your own. Don't wait for others to force you.

- **Bonding of Teammates/Coaches**
  - The bonds built with those you go to battle with will last far longer than the outcome of any game. Make sure you embrace these relationships, enjoy the camaraderie, and emphasize it.
- **Pressure Situations**
  - Learning how to perform when the game is on the line, your team is counting on you, feeling the pressure, and persevering is a unique situation that can offer growth.
- **Rest/Recovery**
  - Allowing your muscles to rest and recover is key, especially during the time of growth and maturation of a young athlete. This time will vary from athlete to athlete and must not be overlooked. Work hard; rest hard.
- **Individual Skill Instruction**
  - Understanding specific skills you need to work on is important if you wish to set yourself apart. Sometimes during peak season it can be difficult for coaches to give the amount of individual instruction each athlete needs. If this is you, seek additional instruction, but make sure you are careful about when your additional training occurs. (Note: The most expensive does not always equal the best.)
- **Fun**
  - It should be fun. It can be fun. Make time to have fun being a kid, it's only a short chapter in your life, and the good times will keep you going when times are tough. Learning that doing things that are "hard" can also be fun is important. If you have zero enjoyment in it, you won't want to put in the extra.

- ➢ **Interaction with Older (or Better) Athletes**
  - It is no surprise that many athletes who grow up playing with their older siblings and their friends perform at a high level. Being around older athletes and/or those that play a level higher will force you to push yourself, see how they handle themselves, and learn from those that have already gone before you.
- ➢ **Levels of Success/Failure**
  - Experiencing success is important, and so is experiencing failure. There's only one way to learn how to respond and move on from success and failure. Experience it yourself. Resiliency will be key on your quest for success.
- ➢ **Varied Use of Muscles**
  - Constant strain on the same muscles can be disastrous for a young athlete. Playing multiple sports, allowing for rest, and using muscles at various intensities are critical. Be smart about the wear and tear put on your muscles before it's too late.
- ➢ **Time Away from Athletics**
  - Sometimes you need to step outside to get a better look within. Doing something else or taking time away for a short time can be important to reinvigorate and remind you what things are important to you and how to move forward.
- ➢ **Mental/Positive Visualization Training**
  - We must train our minds as well as our bodies to perform at a high level. Seek ways to prepare yourself mentally to succeed. Training, books, and positive visualization while training are all important to athletes. Sometimes the hardest place to be is in your own head. Make sure your self-talk is helping, not hurting.

- ➢ **Opportunity to Give Back**
  - It's never too early to start giving back, helping others, and showing your gratefulness. Share with others what you've learned, seek young athletes to mentor, and be the kind of teammate you want on your teams.
- ➢ **Competitive Atmosphere**
  - Depending on the time of year or situation, this can be the real deal or simulated. Learning to be comfortable performing under pressure when competition is high is important. Simulating isn't exactly the same, but you can get close.
- ➢ **Strength Building/Growth**
  - It is critical that you continue to train your body and do the strength building specific to your sport to meet the needs of those muscles. Be careful about when and what kinds of training you are doing as the timing within the progression is important.

The Formula

Once you understand the components involved, it's important to figure out how they all fit together. Putting them in the wrong places, at the wrong times, is going to prevent you from reaching the levels you're trying to get to but also leave you feeling burned out, bored, or despising the time and energy you're putting into being an athlete.

The TM22 Formula—Example

You only get a certain amount of time and energy. Invest it wisely and seek a *dynamic balance*. This adapted Venn diagram/scale illustration helps show where the components "could" fit within the year of an athlete's life. Young athletes will need help identifying these zones, and managing times of transition will play a key role in meeting this challenge.

22—A GUIDE FOR YOUNG ATHLETES

Transition Zone
- Rest/Recovery
- Time Away from Athletics
- Proper Mental/Physical Conditioning/Preparation

Key: Notice the difference in sizes of off/peak season. The offseason is critical in the life of a young athlete.

Off Season
- Build the Dream
- Rest/Recovery
- Individual Skill Instruction
- Fun
- Interaction with Older Athletes
- Varied Use of Muscles
- Time Away from Athletics
- Mental/Positive Visualization Training
- Opportunity to Give Back
- Expand the Comfort Zone
- Simulated Pressure Situations

Core Components
- Hard Work
- Character
- Family
- Education
- Health

Peak Season
- Bonding between Teammates/Coaches
- Pressure Situations
- Levels of Success/Failure
- Competitive Atmosphere

Note: Number of components included will vary between athletes; adapt accordingly. There may also be opportunities to provide components in other phases when time allows. Adapt center of gravity!

Potential Impacts of Negative Imbalance

Injuries—Overuse/not enough recovery time
Burn out—Physically/emotionally
Missed out on acquiring important skills
Poor transitions reduce potential
Core Components impacted negatively
Lack of enjoyment, fun, leads to quitting
Lack of self-motivation, effort not sustained

Potential Impacts of Dynamic Balance

Reach maximum potential
Mentally/physically healthy
Emotionally/socially happy
Equipped with skills and ready for next journey
Appropriate balance of Core Components
Desire to want to improve on own
Sign up again next season

The Foundation

The outcome this formula is working toward is creating a well-rounded, healthy, happy young athlete who has made the most of their time as a young athlete and has come away with the skills, passion, and enthusiasm to continue their success throughout life.

There's a time when each of these components fits. One of the problems with specialization and rise of showcases, AAU teams, traveling select teams, etc. is that it involves peak seasons throughout the year, not allowing for other components to be included within the formula (e.g., rest/recovery). A year in the life of an athlete can be broken into three zones.

Peak Season: Time you want to be at your best. Competitive atmosphere at its highest and should be focused on training. Components such as family, school, and health are still of equal importance, but during this time you may need to counterbalance due to demands of the schedule.

Offseason: Recovery, individual instruction, time to build perspective, strength, and passion toward the sports you are training for. This can be a difficult time to navigate because of the lack of structure, and it is critical that coaches, parents, and teachers give guidance during this time.

Transition Zones: These are the phases in between seasons and training periods that ultimately make whichever model you choose remain balanced. You use these zones to get yourself ready mentally and physically, and this will last for different amounts of time depending on the athlete, sport, health, etc. How you use this time is important, as it allows for specific components to be included even within a full year and allows for a smooth transition between each. The best teachers are those who can master times of transition. *The key is learning the art of transition and how to find the balance between the other zones.*

Tip: You can't be full go all the time. It's not helping you in the long term. Be careful about the impact of club sports and their growing availability and pressure to commit. It's not their fault, but the proper scaffolding and "big picture" of what's best for more than just their club team won't be present. Ask your parents for help in trying to figure out this puzzle.

Model 2: Creating Your Own Compass, Checkpoints, Coordinates

The Challenge/Opportunity: It's common for athletes (and parents) to wish there was a map to follow that showed every path to take, decisions about what to do, etc. The flaw in maps of course is that they imply that there are a few routes everyone should follow. That doesn't really work and is tethering us to one way of thinking. The better approach is to equip yourself with a *compass* that helps you find your bearings from different starting locations and guides you in the right direction; *checkpoints* to help you stay on track and know when choices need to be made; and *coordinates* to give you guidance on where you're hoping all these choices take you.

Important: Trajectory versus Drifting

Before we look at tools that can help us look at where we're heading, it's important to know the difference between determining your trajectory and just drifting along.

Your trajectory is created by choice, not chance. If you don't like it, change it. This doesn't mean you can't be spiritual or believe in a higher power that is guiding where you intend to go. You've still got to take action and make choices that are guiding you in the direction you want. And if you don't like that direction or aren't willing to do what it takes, that's on you.

Most people are content with "drifting" and letting life happen to them.

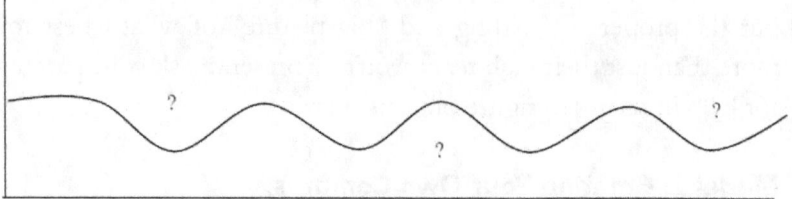

Trajectory is the path something takes through space and time.

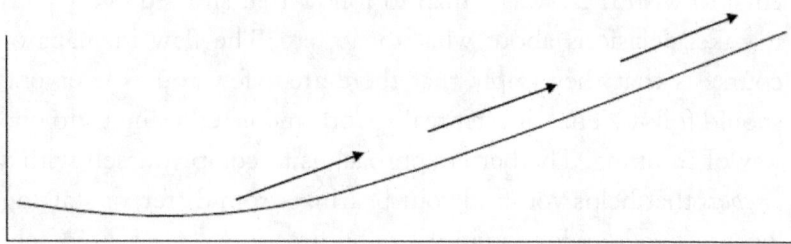

The opposite of trajectory is inaction, off track, distraction, going round in circles, disorientation, or having lost one's bearings. So much is out of our control. Nothing goes exactly as planned, setbacks or small victories; your long-term trajectory is determined by a sustained pattern of actions towards your goal. What can you do to keep your trajectory going in the right direction?

Again, your trajectory is created by choice, not chance. If you don't like it, change it.

The Young Athlete Compass

This illustration is my attempt at creating a compass with the types of components I see being important to athletes regardless of the path they're on. Providing the foundation is perhaps the most underrated of the skills, a moral compass. (Understanding what is right and wrong and the courage to act accordingly. When to take a stand and when not to and why).

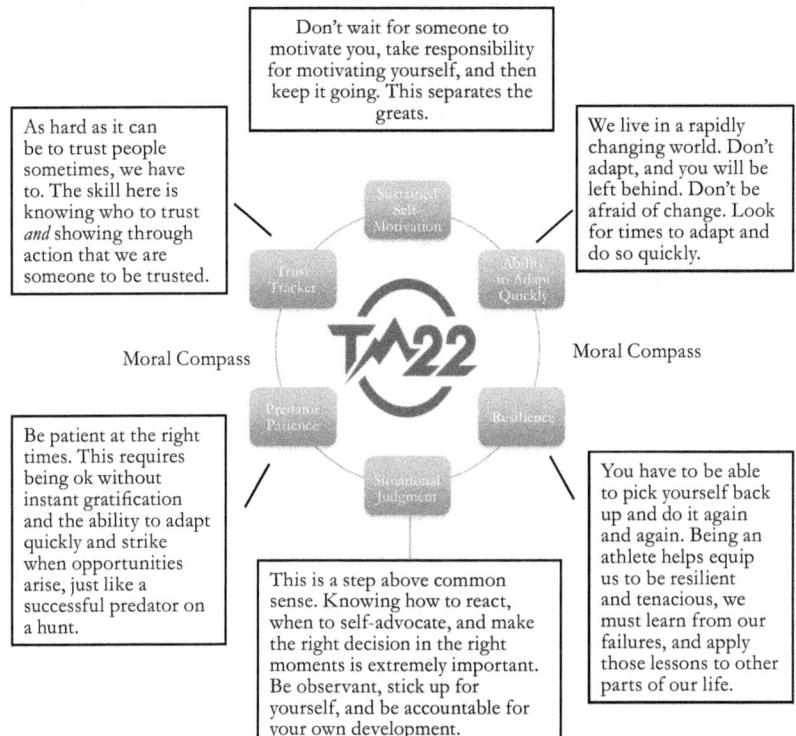

The Checkpoints

There are points along your journey where you need to recalibrate. If you get lost or lose momentum (and you will) or lose sight of your goal, these are designed to get you back on track even when the final destination might change. You really don't have time to take years to get back on track. Here are some examples of questions you can ask yourself at the checkpoints:

- Am I healthy? Mentally and physically?
- Take inventory: Do I have everything I need? Should I ask for help?
- Do my current habits *match the direction* I want to be going in?
- What else could I be doing? Is my routine working?
- How do my actions compare to those around me?

Tip: Setting a schedule to check in and be intentional can help. The key to these "checkpoints" is really to help keep yourself accountable and on track. The goal isn't to try to be perfect; just keep progressing and working toward a goal of your choosing.

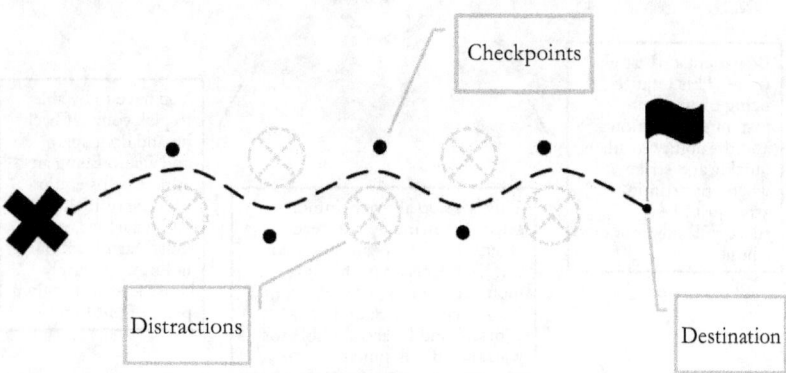

The Coordinates

This can be a goal, how you define success, or a place you want to work toward that, by your definition, is successful. (The key here is that you are at least aiming "at something" and not just drifting.) If you stay disciplined with using your checkpoints and using your compass, you can go anywhere. Be careful when making decisions that can't be reversed, and do it in a timely manner.

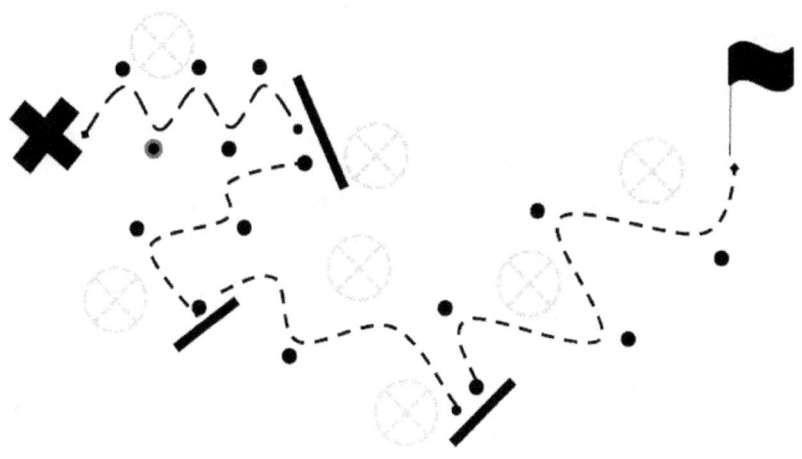

What If the Goal Changes?

It will, and this is why having checkpoints and coordinates is important so you're not just drifting around waiting for life to happen. During difficult times, it's important to recalibrate at checkpoints more often. You are constantly surrounded by distractions, your destination may change, but you will be ready.

Tip: The harder you work, the more doors that will open; do what you can to keep them open and not make choices that close them.

Model 3: Taking Time and Building Dynamic Balance

The Challenge/Opportunity: Athletes that are hoping to reach their maximum potential can't let "not having the time" or "looking for balance" be excuses during this period of life. If it's really important to you, you'll make the time and then find that balance that still allows for productivity.

You don't need me to make a list of all the different things pulling you in different directions, but there really isn't another time in life where you'll be asked to have so many jobs, roles, and expectations, and at the same time those keep saying to you, make sure you keep a balance. So how you do design a life that allows you to do extraordinary things but still find the kind of balance that keeps you healthy and is sustainable?

Tip: *There's no such thing as perfect balance.* I also disagree with the belief that our goal is to live a balanced life or just to "be happy." Life is not easy and can be unpredictable; knowing how to manage times of imbalance is one of the greatest skills you can take advantage of. Being happy is a product of our pursuit of being challenged, fulfilled, and productive. Do those things with integrity, and you will be happy.

> **"The reason we shouldn't pursue balance is that the magic never happens in the middle: magic happens at the extremes. The dilemma is that chasing the extremes presents real challenges. We naturally understand that success lies at the outer edges, but we don't know how to manage our lives while we're out there."**
> —Jay Papasan, Gary Keller, *The ONE Thing: The Surprisingly Simple Truth About Extraordinary Results*

The "Dynamic-Balance" Model

For an athlete, dynamic balance means being able to maintain "healthy balance," but not at the expense of making the magic happen. From the day you are born, life is in motion; those that are willing and can thrive during times of imbalance will be those that achieve their goals. Athletes (and adults) get into trouble when they feel like they can't correct it. This is our center of gravity. If things feel like they are out of control, that's not healthy. Some will be able to operate better than others at the extremes, and it's important for people to know what they can handle.

The Goal: Not seeking a perfect or equal balance of all the elements in our lives, but a deliberate, *self-determined* dispersal of time and energy *appropriate to the situation*—this can only be achieved with intelligent self-understanding.

Key Elements:

- Know your true self. One way to learn about that person is through playing sports.
- Being centered (family, health, etc.) will allow you to reach to the extremes.
- Willingness to take calculated risks, overcome adversity, and feel uncomfortable.
- Keep alignment even when there's lots of external movement.

> **Dynamic Balance**—Its forward leaning, proactive angle is what keeps us moving toward our goals by using a deliberate dispersal of time and energy. The fulcrum (the triangle helping you balance) can be your parents, coach, or friends and can help you, but you need to make it clear you're not looking for easy but rather excellence, and you'll keep enough balance but still be moving forward.

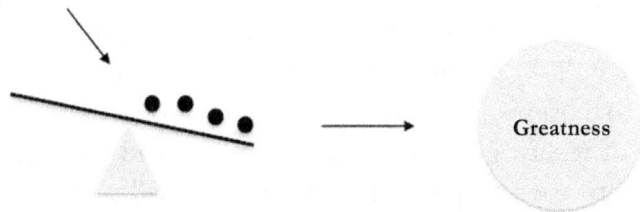

Reminder: This book is for those who want to achieve great things. If you just want to be normal and coast through life, then yes…you should just seek balance.

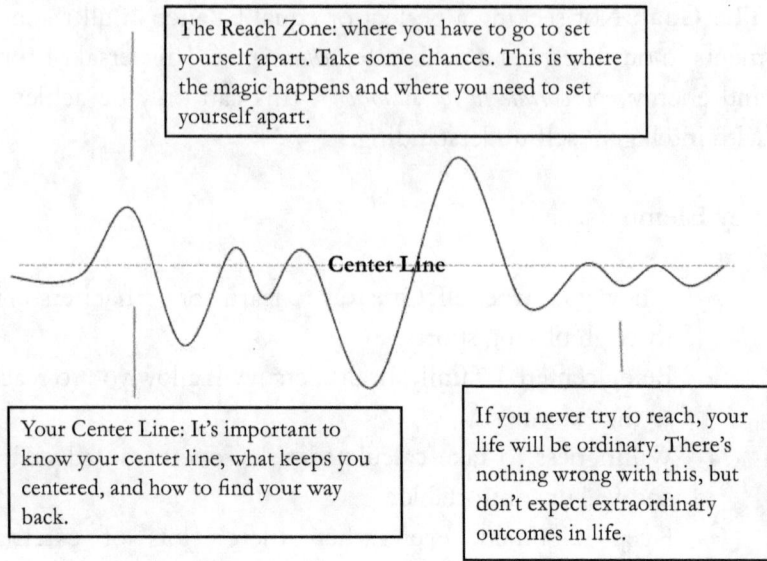

The TM22 Athlete Orbit

When a satellite orbits the Earth, gravity is what keeps it from just drifting away across the universe. It's this same force that's trying to pull the satellite crashing back into the Earth's atmosphere. Too far away, it's a goner; too close, the gravity will be too strong; at the right distance and right speed, it can accomplish some great things.

In the TM22 Athlete Orbit Illustration, you can see what happens to most people who set off on a quest to be great. Some lose sight of reality, goals become nonexistent, and most get sucked back into the strong gravity of being "normal" and conforming. Our structures are set up to suck you in. You go to school, go to practice, get a job, eventually buy a house, and find stuff and people to live in that house with you. These things aren't bad, but they don't have to prevent you (and shouldn't) from doing meaningful, big, memorable things for yourself and others. This force is strong, and you have to be careful not to get too close for too long, or you'll never leave. Somewhere in between is where we want to be. Without losing sight of reality or going crazy, we want to keep pushing ourselves to try new things, be open minded, do things that set us apart, and refuse to let normality pull us back in.

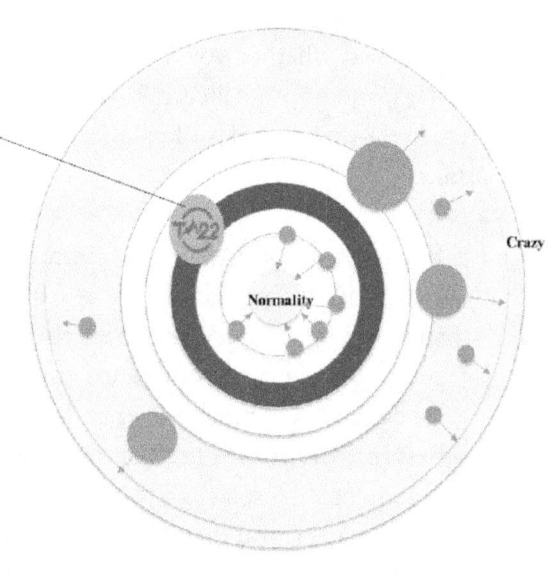

Here's the sweet spot.

While most people will allow the forces of "normal" to suck them in and not let go, and others are lost adrift and have given up on their goals, the TM22 athlete fights to keep moving forward and stay in orbit. Good habits, discipline, and having the courage to dream big will keep you on course.

If you can operate in this zone, anything is possible.

The Concept of Time
Depending on your perspective and how you use it, time can either be your greatest asset or your relentless enemy. It's common for the "lack of time" to be used as an excuse. The truth is, much of that is self-inflicted based upon your view of time and doesn't need to be. Time can also be the greatest healer: "You just need to give it time." It really is a double-edged sword.

In nature, "time" can be important because it can impact the survival of a species—when to migrate, when to mate, when to hunt for food, etc. There are humans who still use this concept of time. It wasn't that long ago that humans would spend most of their day searching for food; it took a lifetime to send information across the planet, and even our life expectancy was fifty years shorter. Here's the point: Don't ever let the excuse "I just don't have time" be something you use. If it is important enough to you, you will make time. And whether you view time as a clock or seasons or moon cycles, you only get a certain amount, so make them count.

Here are some examples of when time is, in our current world, important:

1. **Being punctual:** Show up on time. If you don't, you have no chance at success. There is really nothing worse than showing up late. It's not even about the time; it tells the person you believe your time is more valuable than theirs. Be early. Be on time. Never be late.
2. **Seizing the moment:** You only get a certain number of "moments" to seize. If you miss it, if you aren't ready, if you don't act, you may never get another one.
3. **Life is short:** Our time here on Earth is relatively short. Take nothing for granted. On the day I am writing this, within the past week, my dad had two brothers pass away, and my mother had one. There is nothing like a funeral to remind us of the finite amount of time we get here on Earth. If you "slow walk" everything, you will be quickly missing out.
4. **Quality time:** Playing catch with a young athlete for five minutes is far more powerful than five hours of sitting on a couch with your phone in hand.

5. **Use the pressure of time to your advantage:** Deadlines can be good. Giving yourself too much time to complete a project is going to include lots of comfort, and comfort very rarely breeds productivity. Making and seeing timelines helps me see the big picture in my head and then understand the short actions and deadlines needed along the way.

The good news is that you are in control. Don't let our man-made concepts of time hinder you from doing something epic. Those that make the biggest impact are able to use time as an advantage.

Tip: Don't get left behind waiting for "the perfect moment." There might not be such a thing as perfect timing for anything; having the right mindset will help create the right timing.

Become a Time Master

> "People don't decide their futures; they decide their habits and their habits decide their future."
> —F. M. Alexander

Besides your health, time may be the most valuable tool you have while on this planet. This is a gift you must identify, protect, and take advantage of. Athletes are made up of a combination of talent, hard work, and habits. Do your habits line up with what your goals are?

The following illustration shows how important decisions about how you use your time can be and how your daily habits can transfer to accomplishing big things...or missed opportunities.

Note: The exact times in this model will fluctuate depending on each athlete, but it does average daily amounts of time spent on common activities of young athletes.

A Sample of a Young Athlete Time Map

The map below represents different time usage in the daily life of a young athlete (will vary).

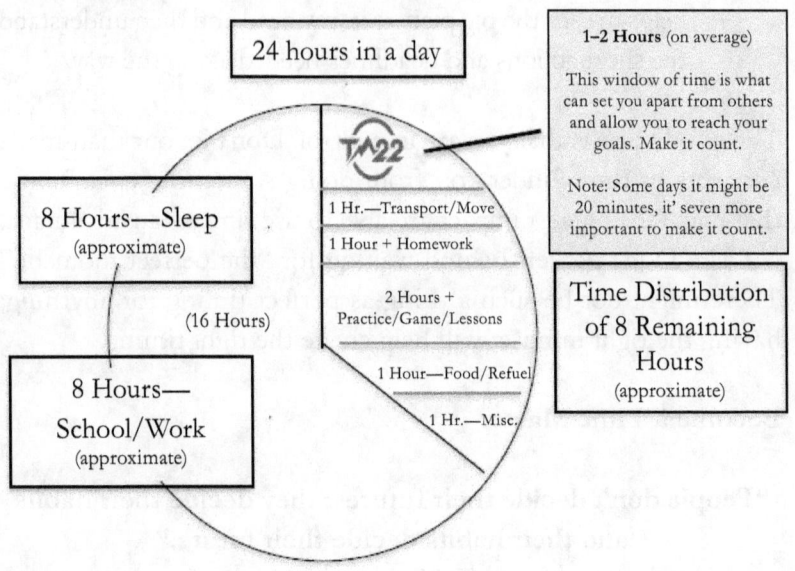

Magic of the Early Morning Window—If you can make it a habit to get up early, it can be the perfect window of calm, clear thinking that you can use that most won't.

Note: This isn't possible if you're staying up until 1:00 a.m.; you also need rest.

> "Early to bed and early to rise makes a man healthy, wealthy, and wise."
> —Benjamin Franklin

Want to know if your daily use of time is matching up with the goals you hope to achieve? Take a look at the steps below.

Step 1: Where do you want to be?
Step 2: Look at the daily energy/time-use chart above or create your own.
Step 3: Does it match up? If you continue to do this throughout the year, what will the result be?
Step 4: Make changes. Follow through.

Tip: Your "lack of time" and the structures that are in place because of sports, school, etc. might be your biggest asset. It gives you the discipline and pressure needed to focus and keep moving.

Time is valuable and can go by quickly. Don't let this worry you; take advantage of it. Learning how to have dynamic balance and master how and what you spend your time on are things in your control and a key part of creating the systems around you that will allow for excellence.

Model 4: Protecting and Promoting Yourself as an Athlete

The Challenge/Opportunity: This generation of athletes is being bombarded from every direction with distractions, media, information, and unrelenting connectivity. Athletes need to be able to not only protect themselves but also navigate tools in a way that they can promote their skills, principles, and the goals they're trying to achieve.

Selfish versus Self-Interest: Who Cares and What's the Difference?

Athletes, especially those who read a book, are often guilty of spreading themselves too thin. We can't help others (team, family, or anyone) if we don't start with ourselves. We want to be good teammates; we want to achieve our goals, but we've also got to take care of our present self.

> **Selfish**—Making decisions that satisfy your own short-term needs but at the expense of others or your own long-term goals.
>
> **Self-Interest (Self-Care)**—Making decisions that satisfy your needs and help your trajectory but still shows empathy and being considerate of others without having a lasting negative impact.

Context: The environment our current paradigm is creating a new, blurry line to navigate between being selfish and making decisions that are good for you in the long term. The number of choices has increased significantly (in general). It's common now for athletes to be bouncing from club team to school team, from showcase to individual instructor; they often overlap, and each has their own purpose and goals. You aspire to play at the next level and know that one of the biggest challenges is getting seen. Your parents, club coach, friends, school coach, and neighbors all have their own opinions, and there really is no easy answer. So now what?

(Note: Examples of scenarios here can range from getting pressured to attend a showcase and missing practices/games with your other team, skipping your school season to stay with your club, or bypassing full seasons just to work out with a personal trainer.)

A Few of the Key Problems:

1. Athletes are making sacrifices that don't match the actual value, perceived and unseen.

2. The adults providing advice to athletes are basing their advice on what's best for them, or what they did, and not what's best for the long-term goals of the athlete.
3. Decisions are getting made without all the right information being present.

(Tip: Ultimately there are times in life when you have to make choices and live with the consequences—that's fine. What you'll regret is that later you discover you didn't have the right advice or info.)

The Path Forward:

1. There's not one easy answer here, and it really depends on the situation, athlete, and team.
2. Whatever you choose, you should give 100 percent of your effort and focus to that team and coach. If you decide at some point that you can't give that full amount, you may need to be honest with yourself (and the other team) about your true goals and commit. Don't mislead; if you're in, be all in.
3. You need to think carefully about the value of what's now and what's next and how those two things are connected in terms of long-term impacts. Is the risk worth the value? Is there another route to that goal with less risk and the same outcome?

A Lens to Look Through

My recommendation to athletes typically includes talking to your parents and your coach and trying to take a long view at the decision that needs to be made. Any adult who really cares about them would say, "If that's what you want and feel confident that's the right choice, good for you." (You also shouldn't undervalue that college coaches or scouts see you willing to commit to a team and the culture you're being invited into, regardless of talent.)

I can't tell you what to do. (And you should be careful about letting any adult outside of your parents do this.) This is so individualized that my advice is to focus on the questions rather than just looking for answers. Here are some examples of questions that will give you the proper lens:

> Does the potential value match the potential impact? How do you know?

> Does your decision have a negative impact on others? If yes, is there a way to lessen the impact?

> What's the motivation behind the advice that you're getting?

> Have you exhausted all options? Did you ask? (Tip: Don't base what you do just off what you *think* some other kid did.)

> Is there someone else who was in a similar position that you could look at what they did? Maybe even ask them? Older athlete?

> Is this a situation where it's more important to focus on what's next or what's now? Which is more important?

Summary: These questions are difficult and another example of why utilizing the adults around you can be so valuable. It doesn't hurt to ask people for advice; you have the courage and humility to do it, and regardless of what you decide, you'll feel satisfied that you did your best to make the best decision you could with the information that you had.

You can't control what happens, and you wouldn't/shouldn't want that even if it were possible, but you should aim to take the right risks. You're going to find out that life is less about what happens to you than how you interpret it, good, bad, or unknown.

Discover Symbiotic Self-Reliance
Self-reliance implies being able to accomplish something on your own. A symbiotic relationship refers to when two things can work together and both entities are impacted positively. This idea proposes that you can do both, and the elite athletes find a way to do it.

You need to watch out for your own best interests and be careful not to sacrifice them for others, but it doesn't mean you can't help them on their quest while also helping your own. When these two paths converge, both can benefit and perhaps become even stronger. Working out together would be an example of improving yourself, but when done together, it has a positive impact on both involved. These two parallel paths are valuable if you can find them.

> Example: Sometimes you can find situations that allow you to help yourself and not have to rely on others, but it also helps someone else do the same. Both benefit. No one is losing for someone else to gain.

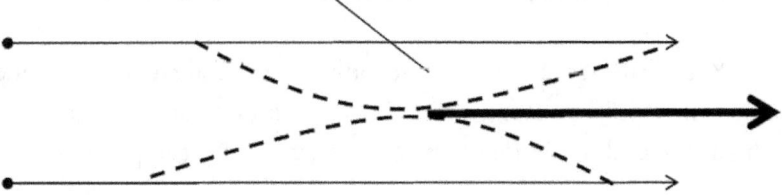

The most successful elite athletes constantly try to surround themselves with other great athletes. Why? Just surrounding yourself with others who have similar trajectories can raise your game. You're not relying on others to motivate you; that's your job, but there's no reason why a bunch of self-reliant, success-seeking athletes can't also benefit from one another, and they should.

Young Athletes: Protect Your Core

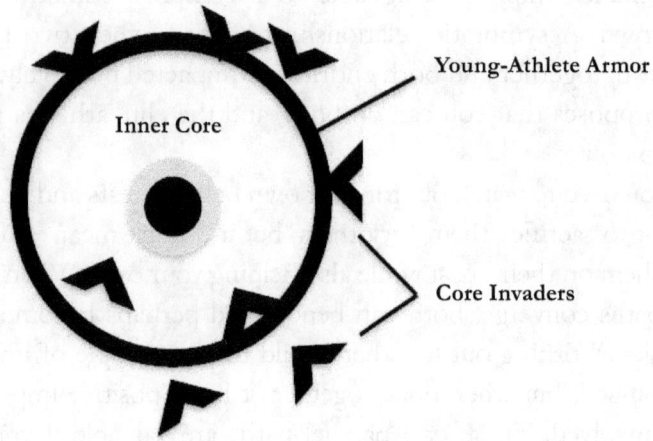

The term "protect the core" can be referenced in movies, in video games, and in battle tactics, but here it is used as a key strategy for achieving success as a young athlete. Your inner core is not an anatomical term; you can't see it, you can't touch it, but you can feel it, and everyone has it.

Your inner core is yours and only yours. You can't let anyone touch it. It is your story, your character, and what you stand for, and at the end of the day, your core is what's most important.

The young-athlete armor is the outer core that people will try to penetrate—sometimes on purpose, sometimes not; sometimes it's a perceived enemy, but it could also be a friend, your cell phone, or even an overzealous adult.

Regardless of what happens to your team and what those around you are doing, you have to protect your core. If you protect your core, you will never have regrets and can hold your head up high wherever you go.

Tip: When self-doubt starts to creep in, I think of those who believed in me and also those who didn't. The biggest mistake that can be made here is allowing someone who doesn't have any footing to impact your core.

Design Your Own Herd
Animals have used different types of "group designs" to survive for millions of years. Whether it's a flock, a herd, or a team, it's important to understand the role you play and what happens when two groups, or "herds," overlap. What makes a flock more than just a bunch of geese? Or herd? Or a wolf pack? Movement.

The TM22 team is *not* just a bunch of individuals looking out for their own best interests; this is a group of athletes joining together to reach the top of the mountain and improve the path for other athletes that will follow.

In a pack, wolves will sometimes have the oldest or weakest wolves travel in the front to set the pace, so they aren't left behind. Geese will take turns being in the front of their V formation, so they can take turns resting and can travel farther. Humans have a unique opportunity to take the herd they were given and make choices on who they want to expand to include. The illustration below shows the difference between your inner herd and those you choose to include.

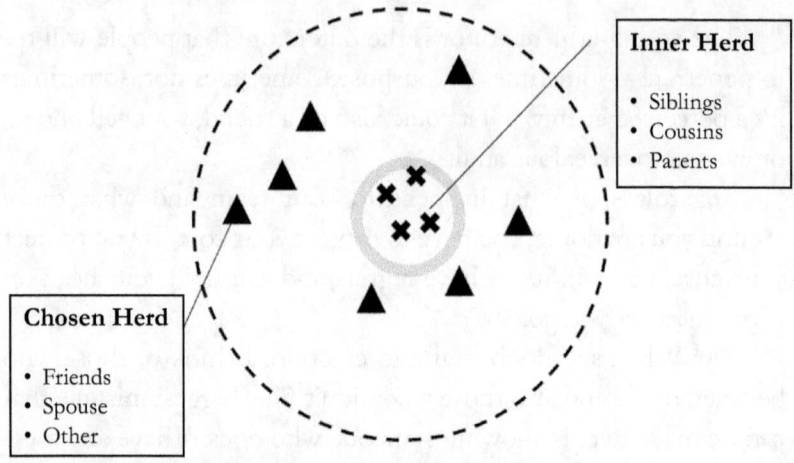

Like your genetics or location of birth, you don't have control of this, but your inner herd must be protected. They are the most important, and even as your chosen herd changes, those in the inner circle will always remain.

When your herd begins to expand and your journey continues, herds will begin to overlap. What role do you play in someone else's herd? Are you helping their herd or someone you would want to let into your own?

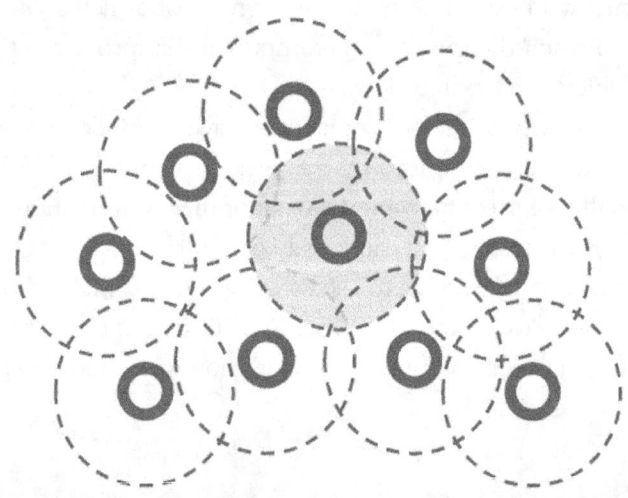

Tip: You don't pick your family; you don't choose your DNA, but you do have a lot of choice about who you surround yourself with. Use good judgment about who this is, and do what you can to protect them and you.

The Social Media Coyote

Coyotes are alert, observant, and masters of knowing when to strike and when to just stay on the periphery. The best athletes can do something similar when it comes to social media.

Social media and the endless number of distractions at our fingertips aren't going anywhere and can be a trap. It's ok to have this, but don't let it consume you; if you can find the balance, it can even become an advantage.

Follow the path of the social media coyote. Stay on the periphery. If you let it lure you in, it will consume you and prevent you from the hunt for success that you are on. Be alert.

Use this distraction to your advantage. Most athletes aren't able to resist the temptation and will let it consume them. While they are distracted by watching the stories of others, you'll be making your own. And don't worry, you'll have your chance to prove people wrong and show your accomplishments in *authentic* ways.

Avoid the traps. Once you post something on social media, it will be there forever. It's like getting a tattoo for all to see, and what you believe as a fifteen-year-old might not be what you do when you're thirty and applying for your dream job. Learn from the early athlete social media users that got doors closed due to a few words they may regret.

It's of course ok if you choose not to have social media, but there can be good things you may want to see or you are able to be reached, and if it's causing anxiety being too far out of the loop, it is an option to be close enough to see but not participate.

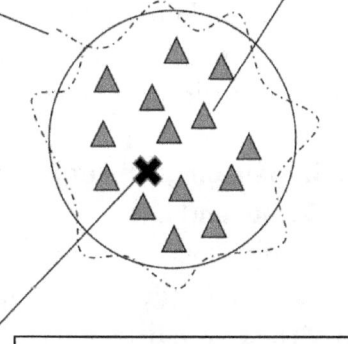

Steps Toward Improving (and Protecting) Mental Health in a Social Media World

1. Understand what's real and what's not, and don't judge your own life against others.
2. It's easy to say don't care about what others think. But you have to constantly remind yourself of whose opinion really matters and ignore the rest.
3. Grow and show self-control. Figure out a way to use its existence to your advantage. Let the others be distracted by it while you get an edge and regulate your emotions.

You need to be able to look beyond the present. Remind yourself that there is a beyond, and yours matters. Social media tricks you into constantly looking at what others have and not focusing on what you have that's real. If in doubt, ask for help, and remember that the best way to navigate this social media world and protect your mental health is to improve your self-awareness and self-control, leverage what you can control, and ignore the rest.

Tip: Theodore Roosevelt said, "Comparison is thief of joy." Be careful of how and why you compare yourself to others. Everyone is different, on their own path, and that's a good thing.

Model 5: Managing Anxiety: Pregame, During Game, and Life

The Challenge/Opportunity: It's becoming a lot more common for athletes to feel high amounts of anxiety and debilitating levels of worry. There's a variety of reasons why this is happening; some are in our control, and some aren't. The controllable section is the focus of these models.

Anxiety Versus Worry: Why It Matters

The previous model talked about strategies to protect and promote yourself; those will be key in helping you during times of perceived crisis or when your anxiety about performing becomes too much. The term "perceived crisis" isn't intended to put doubt in what you're feeling, but it's important to understand the impact we have on how we see a situation, how we perceive it. There is a difference between worrying and anxiety. Worrying is normal, it can be made productive and shows that you care, and you can use this to your advantage. Anxiety is paralyzing—I've seen students/athletes overcome by anxiety without any notice, without any reason I could see—and shouldn't be dismissed. This model is to help you navigate a difficult time, but a good difficult time.

Tip: Control what you can control; do your best not to worry about the rest. Concentrate on the process you went through. Hard work and doing things that make you feel mentally ready can cure all. If you work hard, good things will happen. You control your effort; you can't worry about the rest. The next time you find yourself feeling nervous, anxious, or afraid of the moment at hand, think of all the hard work you've put in.

Here are some things you can do to combat that feeling of being anxious and overwhelmed and use those nerves and feelings to your advantage.

Learning to Be Comfortable in Your Own Skin

You've heard this phrase before. For me it had a different meaning. I had bad acne during high school; there were days my face hurt so bad it was impossible to feel "comfortable" in my own skin. Sports and being on the field provided me with a sanctuary, a place where I could go where my skin didn't matter and no one could really see me. I was only judged by how hard I hustled and what kind of teammate I was; that's all I wanted, and it made me feel good. It might not be your skin that makes the field feel like your safe place, but find comfort in that you can stop worrying about other things and just focus on your sport. It should feel good.

The other hat I wear when I'm not coaching is that of an outdoor education teacher. I'm mentioning here because it probably won't surprise you that one of the best places to turn to if you're having anxiety or stress is nature. It's in our DNA; it's scientifically proven to help, but you can also trust me as a former athlete and current teacher—it works. Keep it simple; don't overthink it; just go to nature. Our brains have been evolving for millions of years; think about what your brain needs, what it's wired to do, and the impact so many artificial stimulants are having on it.

Build Up Your Armor: Mentally and Physically

I found comfort in being ready and chasing away anxiety by doing everything I felt I could to work hard. It gave me confidence to think about how hard I worked in the offseason, in the week leading up to the game, and the sacrifices I made. Regardless of what happened, I knew I had put in everything I possibly could. If you're skipping workouts and "hoping" for the best, it's a lot easier for doubt to creep in. Working hard physically will aid in your mental armor too. A common "stressor" I hear from athletes is the fear of falling behind or not knowing whether there is something they should be doing and aren't.

Strength and Conditioning: How to Avoid the Fear of Falling Behind

The decision to start lifting weights and add different elements of training is one every athlete has to make. The right timing varies for everyone, so how do you know when to start and what to do? I can remember being really concerned about falling behind because my friends had started lifting weights. It seemed like they were growing a lot faster than me. I didn't know what to do or who to ask for help, and it caused a lot of self-imposed anxiety and wasn't necessary. If I could go back and help myself as a young athlete, here would be my advice:

1. **You're ok. You're not behind. Everyone is different.**
    a. Don't compare yourself to others; everyone develops at a different pace. This isn't the training window you should worry about. As you get older, there will be other times where you'll want to start devoting more time and focusing on strength training, and you'll know when that time comes.
2. **Don't be afraid to ask for help. Remember it's ok to be new at something.**
    a. I think I was too embarrassed to ask for help on what to do in the weight room, and I shouldn't have been. Everyone has to learn. There are lots of resources you can find and people who would be happy to help. Watch what other people do, and if you can't do it as well as them at first, it's ok; you'll get better.
3. **Educate yourself about the human body and muscles, and train appropriately.**
    a. When I was in college, I lived with wrestlers and football players. I loved lifting weights, and one summer I got a lot bigger and had never been stronger, but it made me slower and didn't match what I needed in my sport. You have to find the balance. While coaching at Hawaii Pacific University, I had a freshman infielder

who put on twenty-five pounds and, along with it, lost a lot of flexibility. We got him to start doing yoga; he increased his flexibility along with his strength, and he would go on to get drafted by the Yankees. Tip: Don't underestimate yoga.
4. **Some of the best things you can do, you can do at home.**
    a. Push-ups, sit-ups, squats, lunges, exercises with kettlebells, a pull-up bar—using your own body weight is a great way to build strength as your body continues to grow. Don't let the weight room not being open or lack of expensive equipment be an excuse. And don't wait for the "perfect time" to start. Just get the ball rolling, and stick with it.
5. **Be accountable for your own development.**
    a. There is no shortage of resources anymore. You can find workouts on the internet, agility drills, and YouTube videos on weight room circuits, but you have to motivate yourself to go and do it. It is important to do the right things, in the right amounts, or it can result in injuries. It's not someone else's job to motivate you.

Tip: A key difference I see between elite athletes and others is the discipline required for showing consistency and commitment to off-season training. It's easy to go to the gym a few times when it's convenient, required, or you're starting to worry about the upcoming season. The real gains are made in July when your season starts in December and no one is watching.

When I was in middle school, a coach walked by me while I was doing a shoulder exercise, and I remember him saying, "You're going to hit a lot of home runs if you keep doing that." I started doing that one exercise so much it was probably bad for me. What he meant was that if I kept getting stronger, in general, it would make me a better player. Just keep my story in mind if a coach comments on doing a good job on the calf-raise machine—stick to your program.

Help Yourself by Helping Others
This strategy could be as simple as if you're thinking about others, you're distracting yourself from thinking about yourself. It could also be the belief that if you put good in the universe, good will come back to you. Helping others could come in the form of being a good teammate, but it could also have nothing to do with sports. Shoveling your neighbor's driveway or volunteering on a weekend for something you're passionate about—elite athletes often look for things that they can help with and make an impact on. It's a good perspective refresh, lessens the perceived pressure of the performance ahead, and worst-case scenario, someone's day will be better because of you.

Tip: Be intentional about spending more time looking outward than inward. Find something that you care about, do something to help, and it can be a win-win to add to your habits.

Performing When Conditions and Circumstances Aren't Perfect
The best athletes aren't fragile and can perform even when conditions and routines get interrupted. Is it easier when you feel good and everything leading up goes exactly as planned? Of course. Don't be confused and think that the best athletes aren't dealing with these adjustments and are not always feeling at their best. Your bus is going to be late at some point, your pregame meal

might get burned, and you may just feel off, but you still must do your best to use the circumstances around you to your advantage and not let outside forces control the outcome.

Tip: Sometimes it helps to pause and think about what you currently have—what good things are going for you today, as opposed to thinking about the things that could go wrong. We don't spend enough time focusing on the things we have and should be grateful for, but instead focus on the things we don't have and wish we did. Sometimes not getting exactly what you want and having to go through some adversity is just what you need. Elite athletes find ways to use the circumstances around them for motivation, not excuses.

Carry Your Shield, Carry the Trophy

Everybody can play well when they have their A game, but can you still perform at a high level when you only have your B or C game? Everyone experiences some level of anxiety leading up to a big game or at some point during their young-athlete journey, but do you have the tools to overcome it? The illustration below represents a shield you can carry with you. They are all things you can control; they will ensure you have your A game more often and help you overcome anxiety. Games should be fun; if not, you're not doing it right.

22—A GUIDE FOR YOUNG ATHLETES

If you put the time into preparing properly, both mentally and physically, you've done all you can do to get ready. Rest, hydrate, visualize, and be ready and willing to adapt.	Make a routine/good habits and stick to them; if you are on the road, keep as many things the same as you can. Your brain triggers activity in your body without you knowing; the better you can stick to your routine, the better you will perform.

Tip: You control all of these.

Preparation · Routine · The Code · Self-Belief · Work Ethic

You get what you put in; people get what they deserve. I believe there is a code that governs sports; if you are a good teammate, do your best, put in the time; good things will happen, and you create your own destiny.

Think about all the hard work you've put in. If you feel good, you play well; if you play well, you feel good. Give yourself credit, stay humble, play with confidence, and you will be ready for any moment. Believe in yourself, even when others don't.

If you don't work hard, skip reps, and/or don't give 100 percent effort—you will be outed. No shield can protect you, but if you work hard, you have nothing to worry about!

Self-Awareness: An Elite Athlete Secret

Self-awareness may be a word you've heard before, but few know the power or how to unleash it. I always wondered how the best athletes became so self-aware. They just knew they needed to change their pregame routine; adjust their shooting stroke midseason; change their workout routine; know when to push through when tired or when their body needs real rest; understand the difference between being hurt and just sore; when to ask for help; and always be able to make the right decision even when no coach, teacher, or parent was telling them what to do. These decisions are critical, and making a change when it's not needed can be just as harmful.

The best athletes aren't guessing—they know. Most of us increase our self-awareness due to time. Adults have the advantage of the many years that have preceded their current perspective and the mistakes they have learned from, but they also don't have rapidly changing bodies, hormones, and a million other rapidly changing variables.

Gaining this elite, valuable tool isn't that difficult if you know what to look for and understand how the exchange of external input and internal output works.

22—A GUIDE FOR YOUNG ATHLETES

The Self-Awareness Equation

This input includes everything from the outside. It provides you with knowledge, perspective, and options and will give you confidence in your own self-understanding and the ingredients needed to make choices.

Here is what goes in.

External Input

Examples:
- Coaches
- Parents
- Friends
- Social Media

Important: You don't pick all of these, but you do have some control over them. Be selective and understand how important it is to surround yourself with external inputs that will help you, not hurt.

Warning! This is also where anxiety and stress get formed, same combo of inputs. Sometimes you just have to get out of your own head. When in doubt, ask for help.

Your Core
(Head and Heart)

The mixing of external input and your own internal software happens here.

Here's why it's important.

Some call this self-awareness or intelligent self-understanding or self-mastery, but the title is not important—the key is <u>your ability to filter and translate the information that comes in with the internal software only you know.</u>

Note: Self-mastery is never "achieved." Mastery is the act of continuing to perfect. If you've "mastered" yourself, you haven't.

The act of taking on what you've been told, learned yourself, or experienced firsthand and translating that into actions. Your level of self-awareness is shown through these actions.

Here is what comes out.

Internal Output

Examples:
- It's time for a change to routine.
- When to rest, when to push through.
- Start a new workout regimen.
- Make changes in choices of habits.
- Is it a self-fix or time to ask for help?
- Are you right? Are you wrong? Does it matter?
- You can feel your values aren't aligning.
- You paid attention and learned from mistakes other athletes have made.

Does having good external input help? Of course, but even if you could handpick your coaches, teammates, or even parents and get unlimited time to soak it all in, **it's your own ability to pay attention and have the confidence to translate into actions that will complete the self-awareness equation.**

The steps on the following page will help ensure you've got the right recipe of components.

A Few Tips to Improve Your Self-Awareness

Athletes don't have an input shortage. Parents, neighbors, or the internet—there are a lot of places to find input, wanted or not. The secret to being able to take all that external noise, good or bad, and turn that into making the right choices and actions is mastering self-awareness. You interpreted the external input, you know more than anyone else about the other factor (you), and those two factors mixed together will show you how to proceed. Here are some basic steps:

1. **Start with the information only you know and acknowledge you may not know it all**
   What are your strengths/weaknesses? What are your values? What motivates you? What are your habits? Routines? What's going on in your head? Heart? There are things you can see/feel, but you also have blind spots. We all do. Know what you know, and know that you don't know it all, and that's ok. Chemically, developmentally, it could be that you just don't have the tools to complete the equation, but it's not an excuse. Just a reminder that there are elements you don't know and should be aware of that. Just another reason to surround yourself with people you trust.
2. **Pay attention to what's coming in, what's going out, and what to do about it.**
   The purpose of paying attention isn't so that you'll instantly have all the answers and know what to do, but you'll at least have paid enough attention to know that something is off,

doesn't feel right, or that change is needed. Pay attention to not only what you are being told but also what your body is telling you. It's common, especially during peak season, to go on autopilot and stop paying attention to the different things impacting performance. Pause, recalibrate, and if in doubt, ask for help. Remember, not making a decision is making a decision.

3. **Give yourself permission to follow your own instincts and trust yourself.**
Ultimately, it's up to you, and only you, to translate external and internal input and make decisions based on that information. You won't always make the right decision, and that's not a bad thing, but you'll feel better if you are true to yourself. Self-awareness enables self-advocacy. Sticking up for yourself is hard to teach and must be earned, but the more you know about self-awareness, and you keep paying attention, the more you'll understand how the best athletes harness this skill.

Self-awareness isn't just something to be achieved, check the box, and move on. It's a moving target and will be a work in progress until the day we die. Having self-awareness is critical in life, but as an athlete, it is another way to set yourself apart or just survive.

There's a difference between just gathering information and learning something. Having awareness of yourself and how you can take information, internalize it, and turn it into actions is an important process. My hope with all of the information in the den is that it can have an impact on your way of thinking, the lens in which you see problems both current and on the horizon, and have the courage to act.

Bonus: A Tangible Tool to Help Athletes Move Forward

Imagine a program that includes all those people and addresses everything from academics to athletics to individual mentoring. It should be our (the adults) job to create the environment in which a well-rounded, multifaceted experience can occur. This complete model can help every young athlete receive a positive athletic experience *and* reach his or her maximum potential.

If transitions are so key, and we sometimes backtrack when moving on to a new team, or to a new coach, and seasons are so short, what if there was a way we could handle the transitions better? In education, students have portfolios that travel with them, so the next teacher can better understand how to best help them and understand a little bit about their past. What would happen if there was a tool that had the potential to be something you passed on from year to year?

If we look at the goal and work backward, it sheds light on how to get there. In 2015, I began piloting what I refer to as the "TM22 Individual Athlete Game Plan." I selected a small group of young athletes to try it out. Teachers, coaches, parents, and young athletes were all involved in filling out this template. The actual data wasn't as important as the opening of a conversation about doing what is best for the young athlete and being specific about what that meant.

If you choose to do something similar for yourself, you could use the following template as a model to follow and adjust to fit the needs of your situation. The template itself isn't as important as the structure, forecasting, accountability, and mentorship link that will come from it.

TM22 Athlete Individual Game Plan

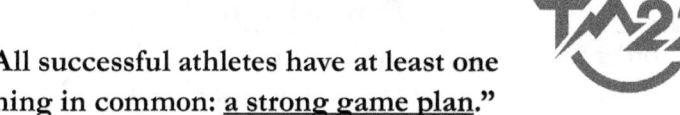

"All successful athletes have at least one thing in common: <u>a strong game plan</u>."
—Lou Holtz

This document is designed for athletes destined to exceed all expectations on and off the field.

Included in this framework is a clarification of purpose, a list of specific goals and expectations, a "roadmap" that will shed light on the athlete's current yearlong progression, and an agreement made by those specifically chosen by the athlete for their support and guidance in developing this plan.

The TM22 athlete is seeking a legacy of integrity, strong character, and resilience. It will be their responsibility to execute this plan, be accountable for their actions, and overcome adversity of any size.

Purpose

Why is being an athlete important to you? What principles do you stand for outside of sports?

Goals & Expectations

Every decision you make will move you closer to or further away from reaching your goals. Use the chart below to set a few short-term goals and expectations as an athlete, student, and person of integrity.

Academics	Character Development	Athletics
In order to succeed on the field, you must succeed in the classroom first. List three short-term academic goals.	List three words/ phrases you want to be used to describe yourself, by your teachers, coaches, and future self.	What are your individual goals this year as an athlete? Key: Create high but attainable goals for yourself.
1. 2. 3.	1. 2. 3.	1. 2. 3.
Plan of Action:	Plan of Action:	Plan of Action:
** Plan of Action: Your plan of action should reflect the steps or actions you will make to achieve those goals. It is the responsibility of the athlete to do the work needed to reach these goals. No excuses allowed. Look carefully at each of your actions, and ask yourself if that is taking you in the direction of the person you're trying to become.		

Athlete Progression Roadmap

This map is designed to illustrate the progression of the young athlete's year. There will be various "moments of impact" along the way, some of which we can't predict and must adapt accordingly. Navigating these moments, taking advantage of transitions, and allowing time for recovery will be critical periods to identify.

	Sep	Oct	Nov	Dec	Jan	Feb	Mar	Apr	May	Jun	Jul	Aug
Academics												
Regular School Year	X	X	X	X	X	X	X	X	X			
Summer School											X	X
Athletics (List Sports)												
Moments of Impact (List notes/ Other Key Events)	Sep	Oct	Nov	Dec	Jan	Feb	Mar	Apr	May	Jun	Jul	Aug

Explanation of Symbols:
X: Months of Peak Season (Athletics or Academics)
___: Offseason Training (Leave blank for coach to write in training phase/progression/individual work)
R: Transition Period (Rest/Recovery)
Moments of Impact/Other: Write in notes of other key events that will take place throughout the year ahead. Example: Tryouts, Showcases, PSAT, family trips, etc.

Coach/Parent/Mentor Note: Every athlete is different. Training progressions, time needed to rest/recover, academic support, etc. will depend on the needs of the athlete. It is our responsibility to help identify these moments of impact and help them understand the level of training needed to reach their maximum potential.

> **TM22 Young Athlete Agreement**
> The signatures below represent the commitment to work together and willingness to adapt accordingly to do what is best for the young athlete on and off the field, now and for their future.
>
> Name of Athlete: _____
>
> **Signatures:**
>
> Athlete: _____ On-Campus Mentor: _____
> Email Address: _____ Email Address: _____
>
> Coach: _____ Parent(s): _____
> Email Address: _____ Email Address: _____
>
> <u>Important:</u> This map, set of goals, and set of expectations should be revisited on a continued basis, and all involved must agree to adapt to help the young athlete succeed on and off the field. For additional support, contact Andy Nelson.

The Outcome

One of the most important results I discovered was the power of just having the initial conversation about the tool and what it made possible. The athletes who helped me pilot the game plan template did a good job filling it out as expected, but it really provided the vehicle to make it clear that a group of people cared about them, on and off the field, beyond just them as an athlete, and there were steps that needed to be taken. It made our purpose clear, and when the athletes asked their parents, coaches, and now mentors at school, it offered a tangible tool to bridge those people together. The information on the paper was important, but not nearly as important as the bond and understanding it created.

This TM22 Individual Game Plan should continue to adapt, be used to keep everyone at the table, and remind those involved that we are trying to do what is best for the athlete here. Remember, you are responsible for deciding who you want to be and where you want to go, and you must take ownership of creating the path to get there. For access to more resources or to contribute your own, "the den" will continue to live and grow at tm22athletes.com.

Conclusion

We have defined what we're chasing, equipped ourselves with new skills, and provided models and tools to overcome them. The next chapter will look at some of the best parts of being a young athlete, how and why you should and can enjoy it, and how you can master leaving regrets behind and taking the good stuff with you.

9

MASTERING THE ART OF BEING A YOUNG ATHLETE

This book is about helping you excel as an athlete. This chapter is about how to take advantage of what makes this window unique and help you master the little things that make it great.

A boy named Shea was one of my best friends growing up. We built forts in the woods, went fishing, and played baseball in the summer and hockey in the winter. If you were trying to start a neighborhood game, your first call was Shea; regardless of weather or temperature, Shea would be in, and if Shea was there, it was fun. Every group of friends needs a Shea.

In August of 2000, I was still recovering from having ACL surgery on my knee and unable to participate in the offseason hockey training. On the way to the rink in Kasson, Shea was killed in a car accident. I have no doubts that, if I hadn't hurt my knee, I would have been in that car, and he would have let me sit in the front. I will never forget the phone call from my friend the night Shea died. To this day, the hardest thing I've ever had to do is help carry my friend's casket out of Sacred Hearts Church.

> "Life is a storm, my young friend.
> You will bask in the sunlight one moment,
> be shattered on the rocks the next.
> What makes you a man is what you
> do when that storm comes."
> —Alexandre Dumas

I ask former athletes this question: "If you could go back and do it all over again, what would you do differently?" The answer usually has a combination of "I would have appreciated the little things more and tried to enjoy it more" and "I think I probably could have worked harder." Figuring out this balance of working hard and being able to identify and appreciate the little things while you're still in the moment is an art—an art you can learn to master.

Tip: We all hope to avoid having regrets. Not taking enough risks is a common regret and a common mistake I see athletes make. Taking a chance and failing will be something you appreciate more than choosing a safe path that protects you from failing.

What Are the "Little Things," and Why Do They Matter?

It is difficult to understand why and how we assign different sizes to things that happen to us. Perhaps it's all based on what others have told us is important, or maybe it's the size of our perspective at the time that has an impact on each event. The key is that the "size" of things will be different for everyone just as much as what those small things are. The first step will be to identify what they might look like, and then we can figure out how to appreciate them.

Only you know the little things that you enjoy the most. There isn't a trophy given out that commemorates your time spent on the bus with your friends, going through "the grind," dyeing your hair blond or growing a sweet mullet, going to battle with your teammates as the marching band plays your school song, standing on the sidelines during the national anthem, wearing a jersey with a name on the back that represents your family, time spent in the locker room, or getting fed after practice at a potluck. It is however these things that you will remember and appreciate for the rest of your life, and you don't need a trophy to remind you.

The little things are also special because they are special to you. At the time, waking up at 5:00 a.m. for mandatory workouts will not feel like something you perhaps enjoy or appreciate, but it will one day be the thing you are most thankful you made yourself go through.

The little things are, in fact, the big things. They are the things that are special to you; you have control of these things, and it is up to you whether you will choose to appreciate them. It may also be the secret to mastering being a young athlete. If you enjoy it, you will fight harder to protect it, and that sustained hard work will be what sets you apart from others.

Tip: The little things are not always good. Sometimes they are tough moments that you will fight to overcome, and because you fought, you will be grateful and appreciate it the rest of your life.

Tips to Take Advantage of Your Time as a Young Athlete

The following tips are ways to help you identify and enjoy the little things more along the way, but also take advantage of opportunities that only exist during this short window of your life.

1. Enjoying What's Now versus Just Looking at What's Next

The key to enjoying the process is being able to identify the things you appreciate the most. This chapter in your life will go by so fast that sometimes you must pause in order to move forward.

Give yourself permission to pause occasionally, look around, and regain perspective on the things you are grateful for. It's common for athletes, especially elite athletes, to constantly be thinking about what's next and lose sight of what's now. Enjoy the now. Everything can change in the blink of an eye, for better or for worse. Be grateful for the moment you are in. It's all you are guaranteed.

2. Timing and Transitions

The best athletes can transition well and identify not only "what" is fun but "how" to have it. Timing is everything. For example, no coach likes the player who is constantly goofing around, laughing, and never focused. You must be aware of the situations you are in and adapt accordingly.

It is also fun to be focused, work hard, and go through hardship. You don't need to have a huge, stupid smile on your face as you run sprints after practice, but inside you should feel happy that you are gaining on your opponents, and every step you take is making you better. This is fun. That weekend when you are at the potluck after the game, wearing a smile and being goofy with your friends is great. Timing and balance of when to have fun, when to be serious, and transitioning well in between are key and will help you enjoy both extremes. Give yourself permission to enjoy being an athlete and all that comes with it.

Also, it's important to note that if your season runs from October to January and you want to be great, the time to work hard is in April or June—don't wait. Use dynamic balance to set yourself apart.

3. Show Gratitude through Genuine Action

When people are in places where their actions can't be seen, their actions will show everyone their true character.

It is often said that the key to happiness is being grateful. Keep reminding yourself of what you *do* have and not what you don't have. If you are healthy, you have a lot to be grateful for. Be happy about this, and see whatever else happens as an opportunity.

The term "paying it forward" is also important. Instead of just saying thank you, show with your actions that you appreciate what someone has done or is doing for you. Help another young athlete, help your family, and be kind to others; this will not only make them happy but you as well.

If you've ever seen a video of an athlete using their signing bonus to buy their parents a house or pay off their mortgage, it's pretty special, but very few of us will have a chance to show our gratitude that way. But if you share the values they taught you and share them with your own children, maybe even better than they did, they will appreciate it; they will also appreciate a house, but this costs less and means more.

Be genuine as you express your gratefulness. Don't wait for someone to tell you to do it. Think about who has helped you and how they did it, then think about what you have and how you could use that to help another. Showing your gratitude will be contagious…and it feels good.

In David Brooks's book, *The Road to Character*, he talks about the difference between eulogy virtues and résumé virtues. This book, much like his, stresses the importance of eulogy values—the things that people will say about you one day. These are based on your genuine actions, how you treated people, and is what people care about.

4. Create Separation—Compartmentalize

One of the things I enjoyed most about being a young athlete was that being on the field felt like an oasis—a place where I could go to get away from all the other difficult things happening during this time in my life. I can still remember how good it felt to run out on the field, stand in the dirt near second base, and know that at that moment, nothing else mattered—just the game.

Do your best not to let various parts of your life run into each other—or "compartmentalize" as best you can. This could mean that if something is bothering you at school, don't let it impact you at practice. If something is bothering you at practice, don't let it impact how you treat your family or how you perform at school. It's not easy, but it's a life skill you'll have to learn to master.

5. Embrace Your Young-Athlete Identity, but Learn to Wear Different Hats

There won't be many times in your life where you are "identified" by the sport that you play. Teachers, neighbors, or relatives might think of you as "the basketball player" or "the soccer player" because it's what you spend so much of your time and energy doing. Take advantage of this and be proud of how you are identified, but it doesn't have to be the only identifier either.

Remember that it is also during this time that people are looking to see your true character. When the day comes when the people in town no longer know you as "the basketball kid" and you are the accountant, they will forget things like basketball and accounting, and just know you for your character. Hey, here comes so-and-so; he is a great person.

It's also important that you learn how to wear more than one hat. This phrase refers to when you're known for having different roles or being passionate about different things. This is important in life; you might get a great job doing a certain type of work, and you do it to support your family, but it might not be your passion. Another "hat" could be doing the thing that you love to do. The key here is finding and following your passion. You can be an athlete, a great musician, and a good brother or sister—learn how to wear different hats.

Be humble, embrace your identity as a young athlete, and use this time to work on building what you want people to always remember you for.

6. When in Doubt, Do the "Right" Thing

This is the first period in your life where you are going to have to make a series of choices that could have a lasting impact on the rest of your life. Deciding what sports to play, where to go to college, and how to train and use your time in the summer are not easy choices. When in doubt, do what you believe to be the right thing and trust your gut.

Small choices like whether to go to a party, which friends you should or shouldn't hang out with, go to a concert or go to a tournament—just do what you think is the right thing. If you do this, good things will happen. Good things happen to those who work hard and do the right thing even when it's the more difficult path to take. Give yourself permission to pause from time to time, think about what you enjoy most about being a young athlete, and do whatever you can to help others have the same opportunity to identify and enjoy those same things.

A character driven elite-athlete trait is being considerate even when others aren't. Everyone leaves a table, there's trash left behind, and you pick it up; you hold the door open for a stranger; you pick up after yourself in a rival school's locker room. These don't seem like much, yet you'll notice that the athletes that excel and get remembered are the athletes that do these things often.

7. Every Experience Will Allow Your Perspective to Grow—Good and Bad

Everything that happens to you, good or bad, is gained experience and will add to your growing perspective. Injuries, getting cut, less-than-great coaches—while you don't want to wish for these things, there is value in overcoming them. Remember—this will be what defines you.

I had ACL surgery on my left knee as a junior in high school. They took a ligament from a cadaver, and after six months of rehab, I was back in action. I am still able to walk because of someone's decision to be an organ/tissue donor. Two games into my junior season of playing baseball at Augsburg College, I could feel that something was wrong. After a month of testing, doctor appointments, and being thirty pounds lighter, I was diagnosed with a liver disease. I would spend many hours that year in the hospital. There is nothing like an injury or illness to shed light on the things that you really appreciate.

One day your ability to overcome these obstacles will mean *more* than when times were easy. Embrace adversity, and it will help you appreciate the little things just that much more. Life isn't always fair; it doesn't have to be. Don't be surprised when you encounter difficult moments, just respond with a positive attitude, and take one step at a time.

8. Have the Courage to Ask Those Who Have What You Want

This is how it all started for me. I wanted to learn. I wanted to be the best I could possibly be. So, I started to ask others that I looked up to, respected, and wanted to have what they had. Ask the people around you what they enjoyed most about being young athletes. People generally like being asked for advice and will take it as a compliment. You may also receive advice you didn't ask for and need to glean what you can and try to understand if it's advice worth taking.

Tip: Don't be afraid to ask and choose people who you respect and who have the types of things and lives that you want. You'll be surprised by what can come from just learning to ask the right way.

9. Create the Environment for the Memorable Things to Occur

This means that it is up to you to create the right conditions for positive things to happen. Be a good teammate, include others, and be open minded and willing to create memories and not just wait around for someone to give them to you. Surround yourself with the right people, be creative, and keep reminding yourself that it doesn't matter what has been done in the past or what others are doing—this is your story.

Tip: Pay attention. Animals that have survived, evolved, and are still successful are those that pay attention to their surroundings. Young athletes have so much happening around them all the time that it's really easy to get stuck on autopilot and just let things keep coming. You might have to be intentional about creating environments and time that are the habitats of good memories.

10. The Moments: Identify and Enjoy the Good; Overcome the Bad

When I was a kid, my dad gave me Richard Carlson's book, *Don't Sweat the Small Stuff, and It's All Small Stuff*. I remember it being a tough time, and I was struggling to gain perspective. This book helped me gain a heightened appreciation for what I had and encouragement to not worry about some of the things I had no control over and in the big picture really didn't matter.

Don't let the small "bad" things weigh you down; overcome them and move on. What you're experiencing now won't always be, big and small things. Work hard at identifying the difference, and don't worry about things like the opinions of others. There is really nothing better than going to battle with your friends and coaches playing a game that you love. Don't take it for granted. No one tells you this the last time this group of people will ever be in a lineup, on a team, or the last tome you'll even see each other. The lesson here isn't to be sad but appreciate the moments and be present.

Tip: Take pride in your name and where you came from. Both things you don't control or choose, but you do represent them. You have the power to change how people view those things just by the things you do, not say. That's an awesome opportunity and responsibility that most don't realize until your days of wearing a jersey with the name of your town and your family are behind you. What other place or chapter in your life has this?

As Your Path as a Young Athlete Nears an End...

Eventually, it all comes to an end for every athlete. The hard times and the good times, they are now just memories that combine to create a chapter in your story. While there is no denying that it can be a sad day when you realize your days of being a young athlete are over, the good news is that you will feel great about all that you accomplished and have a lot to look forward to. No one can ever take away what you overcame and the footprints you left behind. When your time as a young athlete has come to an end, will you be able to say these things?

- I was a good teammate and when I left the program, it was in a better place.
- I contributed positively to those around me beyond just those in my sport.
- I made mistakes but did my best and never stopped seeking to improve.
- I had the courage to take risks, make sacrifices, and overcome adversity.
- I will be remembered for striving to do the right thing and having integrity.
- I did my best to be accountable for my own development and growth.
- I didn't let someone else determine my destiny as an athlete. I was myself.
- I didn't always win or succeed, but I put it all on the line and am proud.
- I had a good attitude and took responsibility during times things didn't go my way.

Note: Whether you're reading this with ten years of being an athlete remaining or two weeks, it's not too late to change, make things right, and end things on your terms. You can't control how, when, or where this chapter ends, but you can control your effort and how you apply the experiences you earned.

The next chapter looks at what the land beyond the young-athlete mountain looks like and how to make sure we're ready. Understanding what that means now will help you when that time comes.

"Do not confuse a life of comfort and ease for the good life. The good life is one of pushing your boundaries, incrementally overcoming yourself, striving for greatness—whatever that means for you. The happiness that results from the absence of discomfort is the happiness of mediocrity.

"Live your life, not as if you were trying to hoard a precious treasure, but as if you were crafting your own autobiography with every decision—because you are."

—Ryan A. Bush, *Designing the Mind: The Principles of Psychitecture*

10

THE LAND BEYOND THE MOUNTAIN

All athletes know that, at some point, it all comes to an end.

The last time you put on a jersey, the last time you play an organized sport, the last time you get to stand and listen to the national anthem with your teammates, get your name announced, have an arena of people there to watch you—this isn't an easy transition, but it's better when you don't have regrets and are prepared for what comes next. The TM22 philosophy applies not only to being an athlete but also in the life that follows by design; it should become a habit. Whatever path you choose, do your best, do it with integrity, help others along the way, be accountable, and if you don't like the path you're on—change it.

A mistake I see athletes make (and have learned for myself) is not seeing the proper preparation being done while still being an athlete. You can (and should) take advantage of your time as an athlete to make sure you're ready and be ready to set yourself apart again from those same athletes that started with you at the bottom of the mountain who are also now looking for what's next. This transition is important, an opportunity, and is the focus of this chapter.

> Important: The point of this chapter isn't to encourage you to start worrying about your career or what comes after high school; it's the opposite. Gaining perspective now should allow you to be present but also help you forecast. When the time comes to move on to what's next, remember this chapter, and come back to it.

No More Metaphorical Mountains

One morning I peered out the window while eating breakfast at the Open Café in Palmer, Alaska. Palmer is a small town nestled against the Matanuska River and the edge of the Chugach Mountain Range, approximately forty-five minutes north of Anchorage. It was spring, and the mountain was beginning to thaw. Tall, majestic, rugged, inviting, scary, and beautiful: this was no metaphorical mountain. If you are willing to leave the safe confines of the café, you can find a path leading toward the top. It is not without dangers, and many who consider the climb are deterred by things like time, exhaustion, and even the good possibility of crossing paths with a bear. It isn't the view on top of this mountain that you take all these risks to see. It is what lies beyond.

On the other side of this first peak are five hundred thousand acres of mountains and wilderness, a third of which is covered by active glaciers ripping through the bedrock of Eastern Alaska.

Mount Marcus Baker is the tallest peak, reaching over thirteen thousand feet; this rugged landscape wasn't formed by getting coddled by Mother Nature. It is three hundred miles of patience and perseverance and home to endless opportunities, dangers, joy, and adventure. It is the land beyond the mountain.

This book begins with a story of young athletes climbing a mountain that symbolizes the pursuit of reaching their goals. Eventually, whether at the summit or somewhere down below, all will be forced to venture beyond into a place we refer to as "the land beyond the mountain." This is life beyond sports. This place contains many unknowns. There will be new challenges, and new trails will have to be blazed. Fortunately for young athletes, there is no group better equipped for the paths ahead. All the time, hard work, resilience, and overcoming adversity have equipped them to overcome any obstacle and pursue goals set atop the summit on even higher mountains.

Locate Your Guiding Star and Never Feel Lost

Very few athletes know when and how exactly it ends, so it's hard to prepare. It's how you've identified most of your memory-making, friendship-building, and decision-making lives. A lot of structure and routines are instantly changed, and most athletes will feel some level of uncertainty of what lies ahead.

When you're trying to figure out what's next, worry less about the exact job, money, or title and seek areas you're interested in continuing to learn about, want to change, or just genuinely care about. Your next path doesn't mean it needs to last forever, but you won't regret devoting time and energy toward something important to you and doing it for the right reasons. This is the time to be opening doors and going through them, not looking for ways to conform.

So what's a guiding star? Have you ever heard the phrase "follow the North Star" or "the North Star of our organization is…"? In our current sky, the North Star is a star called Polaris, and it doesn't move, at least during our lifetime. Why? It's on the same axis as the North Pole. It's what travelers and explorers often seek for a reliable directional tool. This star isn't the brightest, but it's reliable.

(Tip: Find Your Guiding Star. This means finding something you're passionate about that *you want to* pursue. Even if you fall short or something changes, you'll land in a spot you're proud of and can avoid a lot of confusion, anxiety, and discontent. Earlier we talked about defining success and the importance of choosing to pursue excellence. This is addressing what that thing is beyond sports and can help provide a direction to align your habits around.)

How to Find Your "Guiding Star"

This set of stars is known by most as the Big Dipper. Think of these seven brightest stars as the people that you admire. Regardless of whether you can see the path ahead, use the reasons why you admire those people to help guide you in the direction you'll be proud of. Worry less about the specifics of a job, the money, and focus on what they taught you and what path they would encourage you to go in.

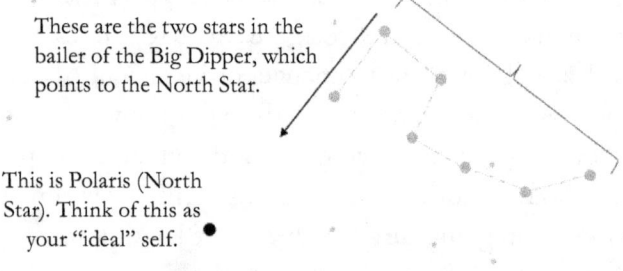

These are the two stars in the bailer of the Big Dipper, which points to the North Star.

This is Polaris (North Star). Think of this as your "ideal" self.

A Few Voices from Beyond the Mountain

One of the questions included in my ongoing research and data collection is, "What do you think young athletes need to know about the days after being a young athlete are over?" Here are a few of the themes athletes have shared that stood out to me.

- ❖ **Don't Worry About Having Everything Figured Out**
  It's common for athletes or any soon-to-graduate senior to assume they need to have everything figured out the second they receive their diploma. Where you will be working for the next fifty years, who you might start a family with, where you'll live—these huge life events are important, but the bigger regret will be attempting to rush, force, or paralyze yourself over them. Use the skills you've been acquiring as a young athlete to keep making good decisions, take risks, and pursue what you're passionate about and that your principles will allow you to chase. You have time; you don't have to be perfect; don't worry about having everything figured out. No one does.

- ❖ **If You Want It Bad Enough, Anything, or Most Things, are Possible**
  A lot of people say they want to be successful; few are willing to do the work and make the sacrifices needed to actually get it. Don't let anyone tell you something isn't possible; you just have to want it bad enough, put in the work, and have the courage to do something about it.

- ❖ **Learn to Find the Positives in the Negatives**
  In any situation, as bad as it might be, look for the positives. This doesn't mean we should pretend that really bad things are actually good things and we should be thankful, but life beyond sports is full of situations that require us

to look for the silver lining, even if they are difficult and small.

- ❖ **No One Has All the Answers**
  Your parents, coaches, teachers, and all the other adults you know may seem like they have all the answers, but they don't. Nobody does. There is a lot we don't know, and all we can do is do our best to prepare ourselves for when that time comes. It's ok not to know the answers, it's ok to say I don't know, and it's ok to understand that we are in this together.
- ❖ **Relationships: Set High Standards**
  Life is too short to spend any of it with someone who doesn't appreciate the time and energy you are giving them. Don't sacrifice your goals because of somebody else. Find someone who will encourage you to reach your dreams, help them reach theirs, and don't settle. On the other side of this, make sure you're doing your part in continuing to be a "good teammate." It's not all about you; find ways to help those you're spending time around to reach their goals, feel supported, etc.
- ❖ **Never Stop Pushing Yourself Physically and Mentally**
  Find ways to keep pushing yourself, it might look different, but it's important to keep learning and finding ways to challenge yourself physically. You might not have a race, an event, or a team you're training for, and instead the focus shifts to taking care of yourself so that you can take care of those you're responsible for. If you feel good and keep telling your brain you're trying to grow, you will be able to think clearly and avoid having any physical obstacles from reaching your goals. Keep reading books, listening to speakers, taking classes, etc. The

more knowledge you have, the more you will enjoy the things around you.

- ❖ **Don't Be Afraid to Do Things Differently: Take Chances on Things You Believe In**
  The world is set up in a way where it will try to suck you into existing systems. If you let it, you'll find yourself doing what everyone is doing, in the same ways for the same reasons, and one day you'll retire, and that's it. There's nothing wrong with this, and we're not entitled to having a long life that ends in retirement, but you'll be grateful if you were willing to take some chances along the way and do things differently.

- ❖ **Life Can be Tough and at Times Unfair—and That's Ok**
  Life can be unfair at times, no matter how you look at it. Some people get more breaks than others, things are going to happen to people that you know that makes no sense, family relationships can be messy, and no matter how hard you try, there will be events that just can't be explained. Luckily, your time as a young athlete has helped you with the skills and grit needed to overcome anything, even if it may seem unfair. Not all times of "unfairness" are bad.

- ❖ **There's a Difference between Good Stress and Bad Stress**
  The goal should not be to have a stress-free life. It's important to learn how to identify and manage stress, know the difference between worry and anxiety, and do what you can to use stress to your advantage. Spending a lot of time worrying about what others think or things that you can't control is not a good use of your mental/physical energy and can have a negative impact on your health.

Stress can be channeled positively and help you achieve great things.

Tip: If you ever find yourself in a place you can't overcome alone, ask for help. One key difference between worrying and anxiety is that worrying about something can be productive if you harness that stress into being focused and prepared. Prolonged stress (worry that lasts a long amount of time) or anxiety (where your amount of worry is paralyzing you from being able to function) are things you really need to ask for help with. Your parents are a good start, but the best athletes also talk to doctors and other experts that have the right tools.

❖ **Don't be Afraid of Transitions: Be Good at Them**
Life is full of transitions, some big, some small, some of our own choosing, and some not. Those who can master them will be the most successful. Things also don't always line up perfectly, and you'll have to transition for different amounts of time and in different ways—one job to the next, relationships, homes, inning to inning, season to season. The key is learning to thrive in these times of transition. The good news: there is no better place to learn this skill than in sports.

The following illustration mimics something you would see on a bike-workout screen. If you work hard and prepare yourself for transitions, you will be ready for the next. There will be lots of transitions needed throughout life and varying amounts of stress, and that's ok.

22—A GUIDE FOR YOUNG ATHLETES

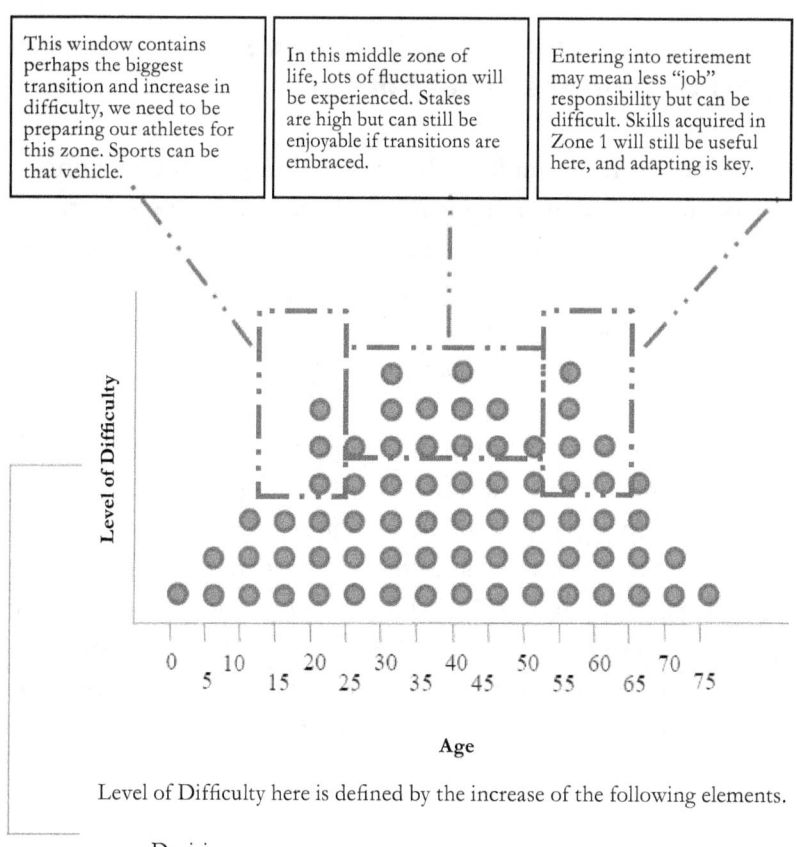

Level of Difficulty here is defined by the increase of the following elements.

- Decisions
- Pressure
- Stress
- Responsibility
- Consequences of Choices

Transitions are critical—in training, at school, and at different stages in life. Some of the biggest transitions are going to be from high school to college and from college to life as an adult. In the land beyond the mountain, many of those who helped you identify when and how to transition won't be there to guide you. Embrace the challenge, appreciate the changes that come with it, and continue to find ways to set yourself apart.

Making Important Decisions in the Land Beyond the Mountain

> "The ability to make deliberative, long-term decisions is one of the few truly unique characteristics of Homo Sapiens, right alongside our technological innovation and our gift for language."
> —Steven Johnson, *Farsighted: How We Make the Decisions That Matter the Most*

Again, your life is a connected series of choices and decisions. We make choices every day whether we know it or not. Even not making a decision is a decision. Some choices we make limit or eliminate future options, and some create more, better options. The key to winning "the game of life" and achieving whichever destination you desire is to make the right choices at the right times (or sometimes make the best out of a bad decision). The choices you make during your young-athlete window are important but will be even more important in the land beyond.

22—A GUIDE FOR YOUNG ATHLETES

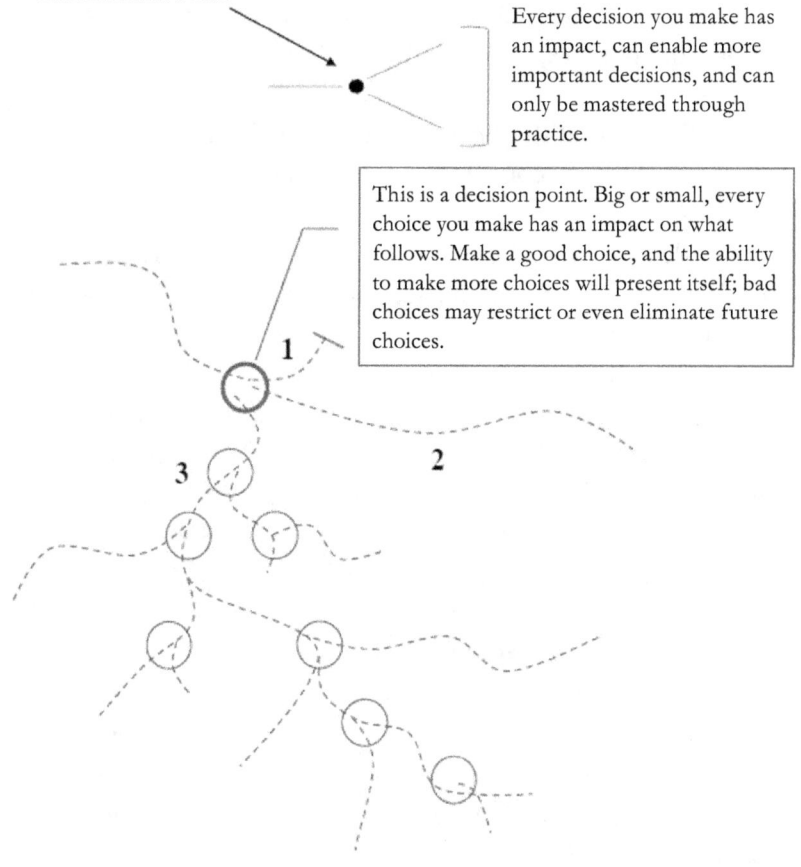

The Decision Point

Every decision you make has an impact, can enable more important decisions, and can only be mastered through practice.

This is a decision point. Big or small, every choice you make has an impact on what follows. Make a good choice, and the ability to make more choices will present itself; bad choices may restrict or even eliminate future choices.

The decision point above indicates that you've had to make a choice about something. Down path 1, you can see that the choice was a poor one, resulting in a dead end. Path 2 shows that while you were able to proceed, your choice narrowed future possibilities and will be restricting. And on path 3, you can see that not only is there room to continue on but also a chance for many more decision points down the road.

According to Ray Dalio, author of *Principles*, in order to have the best life possible, you have to:

> **1) Know what the best decisions are, and 2) have the courage to make them.**

Take pride in learning how to make good decisions. Don't let one bad decision in your past impact your ability to make good decisions in the future.

Tip: We all make bad decisions; learn to move on from those you can't change; don't let the future cause you anxiety and do what you can with the present. *Start acting, thinking, and doing those things, and you will start to become that person.* If you want that better tomorrow, start working on it today. Here are some other areas where you can set yourself apart in your life after sports.

The Power of Thought

One of the things that sets humans apart is our ability to think creatively. Don't let that go to waste, and make sure you are allowing your brain to maximize its power. For example, sometimes doing things like going for a walk can help provide the mental space to make a difficult decision. Many of the world's greatest thinkers throughout history all hold in common their habit of going for walks. It allowed them to think on a higher level and with a clear mind.

Past, Present, and Future: How to Divide Up Your Time/Energy/Thought Investment

What's the proper percentage of time/thought/energy to be spent thinking about the past, present, and future? What if you spent just a small part of every day thinking about what's ahead? Not worrying, just thinking about it. If it's big, it will need the right amounts of time, thought, and energy—like a recipe.

The Past: 5 Percent

It's true that we shouldn't dwell on the past, worry too much about things beyond our control, or let our past define us. I'm not stuck on 5 percent, but I know it can't be zero. Our past gives us perspective, we shouldn't forget where we're from, and it helps us avoid repeating mistakes that will make our present lives better and future paths still possible.

The Present: 85 Percent

This is the only option that we have direct control over. Our actions will define what lies ahead, and it is important to enjoy the present, as nothing beyond this is guaranteed. However, it's important to note that we can't live our day-to-day lives just by completing checklists and not thinking beyond what's standing in front of us. Be present, but don't do it with blinders on.

The Future: 10 Percent

Nothing is guaranteed, but you do have an impact on what options you might have and can set yourself apart if you're thinking ahead. Your present does not need to be sacrificed because you are devoting time/thought/energy to the future; in fact, it's a good investment. Thinking about what it is that you want and what you need to do to get there will leave you better prepared to create your destiny and not just let life happen to you.

Gain an Edge by Gaining Time: Do the Math

If you can make it a routine to wake up an hour earlier each day and use that time to get work done, think, and be productive in an area that you're passionate about, think of how far ahead that's going to set you apart from those after the same goals. Here's the math: 5 more hours a week (minimum) x 52 weeks in a year x 10 years of being a young athlete and setting yourself up for the life beyond being an athlete = 2,600 hours = 108 days of "extra" time you've created that most athletes aren't getting during this critical window in their lives. That edge can be yours with just a little bit of discipline.

Note: This doesn't work if you're on your phone until 2:00 a.m. each night and are just waking up to scroll through your phone for an extra hour. If that's the case, go back to bed because rest is more helpful, and this will be an opportunity for someone else who wants it more. The key is really about how you're spending that time, not the amount. It doesn't have to be every day. There can be events that disrupt routine, but don't use holidays as your excuse. That's what most will do. That's a chance to set yourself apart. Think hard about the reason you're taking the day off or straying from your plan.

How *You* Can "Change" the World

This book is designed to help your current quest as an athlete, but this book is also for the type of young athletes that aren't content with just being successful young athletes. They want more. They want to leave a mark. If you are 11 years old and aren't quite ready to take on the world, it's ok. Start by figuring out what it is that you care about, and then find a way to do something about it.

Tip: When I refer to changing the world, don't underestimate what a small impact on someone else's life you can have.

Making a positive impact, on whichever path you choose, is possible.

When we were talking about being the best athletes, we watched the athletes that came before us closely. If we're looking at finding ways to leave our impact on the world, we should look closely at the people who had an impact we'd like to replicate on the world around us.

> **"Identify the experts, the next step is to figure out specifically what they do to separate themselves from other, less accomplished people. And what training methods did they use to get there."**
> —Anders Ericsson, *Peak: How to Master Almost Anything*

From explorers to civil rights leaders to humanitarians to my own grandma, there were lots of differences, but the similarities these humans all have are what's worth recognizing. Here are a few of the "variables" they all possessed:

- They accepted the challenge.
- They overcame hardship, experienced adversity, were resilient, and moved forward.
- They were different than others, and they were ok with it.
- They spent a lot of time thinking and had lots of ideas (not all good).
- They may have had several interests, but a focus on one specific thing was greater than others.
- They experienced fair amounts of failure and ignored lots of naysayers.
- They possessed the desire to be a part of something bigger than themselves.

- They were willing to sacrifice being comfortable with instability and change.
- They were ok with not following the pack, blazing their own trail, and refusing to be ordinary.
- They recorded thoughts/took notes (most had notebooks in one form or another).
- They were persistent, self-motivated, and sustained efforts over time. They were tenacious.
- They had a strong belief in themselves and their passion.
- They had the ability to forecast and see things before others could.
- At least one person encouraged them to keep going.
- They could handle anxiety in times of crisis and didn't allow self-doubt to take over.
- If they didn't like the way something was, they did something about it.

Perhaps most importantly, they all had different forms of "grit," which is defined by Leonard Mlodinow in his book, *The Upright Thinkers*, as "the disposition to pursue long-term goals with sustained interest and effort over time."

It's true that people who make an impact aren't usually fools, but they aren't all geniuses either. They just spent a lot of time devoted to thought and "deliberate practice" in an area they're passionate about. Many of their ideas weren't great; they failed early and often, but they weren't afraid of change, and some of their ideas turned out to be world changing. These examples help, but it's important to note that in order to get your message across, you will need a combination of enthusiasm, hard work, self-belief, and some good risk-taking, *which might be unique to only you.*

Tip: Don't discredit small, positive actions and acts of kindness. Making a difference in just one person's (or even an animal's) life could change the world. You can change *their* world. Don't underestimate the power of any small, positive action on another's life.

How to *Change* the World: A Proposed Equation

There's an infinite number of ways you can have a positive impact on the pocket of the world and time you live in. Some are athletes, some are not, but they all seem to follow the same basic equation. Don't focus as much on the elements of math as you do on the factors.

Most people accept the status quo and will complain about any type of change. A lot of people have become good at saying they will do what it takes, but in reality very few are willing to take the risks and make the sacrifices needed. Add it to the list of why learning decision-making skills and resilience through youth athletics is so important. Gary Keller and Jay Papasan wrote a book titled *The One Thing: The Surprisingly Simple Truth About Achieving Extraordinary Results*. In the book, they state "the truth about success is that our ability to achieve extraordinary results in the future lies in stringing together powerful moments, one after another." Work hard to create those moments and be the kind of person who is willing to make a positive change in this world.

Equation:

Positive Growth (Adversity Event(s)) + Focused Thought/Research/Practice/Attention (Area of Interest or Passion) + Action (Opportunity + Timing) = Moment of Impact

Explanation:

Adversity Event(s)
Remember how important we said struggle was to humans? Most will experience some level of adversity at some point early on in their lives. Those that can not only overcome but also leverage those experiences into positive growth will acquire the important skills needed to complete the next phase (e.g., grit, resilience, accountability, decision-making skills, discipline, sense of purpose, sacrifice, perseverance, etc.).

If you listen closely to what people say when accomplishing something big, they will always mention how important the people around them are or the important role their "supporting cast" plays. This is no coincidence, and it makes overcoming adversity possible.

Focused Research/Practice/Attention in Area of Interest
Once you have found an area that interests you and you become passionate about learning more, we can again apply Ericsson's concept of "deliberate practice." Out of this focused attention, practice, and research come new ideas, thoughts, and the desire to know more. It is important that the skills learned from leveraging adversity are added to this, or the equation will be incomplete. You must also be careful not to try to do too many things.

Action (Opportunity + Timing)
Equipped with the skills needed to keep moving forward with devoted thought in a particular field/area brings us to the next part of the equation. There will eventually be an opportunity, and when the timing is right, we must take action. If we take action, it

will result in our moment of impact. This is where a legacy is left and changes to the world can be made.

Moment of Impact
If you are properly equipped and if you are ready and willing to act, you can make lasting change. This part of the equation may require you to share your bold ideas. Your self-belief will be tested; don't let anyone take this moment from you. Remain steadfast. If any of the parts of the equation are missing, you may miss out on your moment of impact.

Warning: Do *not* let distractions cause you to miss your moment. It is a growing trend that humans are floating through life on autopilot. Not devoting enough time to thought is a critical mistake (e.g., all the hours spent mindlessly scrolling through pictures will add up. Learn to control your use of technology, or you will lose your chance to make a difference). How to identify moment of impact: In most cases, Carson Daly is not going to announce, "Come on out; this is your moment!" You have to be looking for markers or indicators that show that, if you take action, something big could happen. You might be nervous, excited, or even afraid, but you know that if you attack this moment unique to only you, that's how legends are made.

Summary: Our ability to leverage early events of adversity into positive personal growth is key. Without these acquired skills, the equation won't go much further. It's important we're not robbing our athletes of attaining these skills. Do whatever you can to seek ways to involve yourself with things you can't accomplish alone and with things you can't accomplish in your lifetime.

How to "Change the World": A Proposed Path

The following progression illustrates the various phases that those who have made a difference throughout history have followed. Pay close attention to the elements that each phase contains and does not contain. Leaving a legacy and lasting change isn't easy, but this might be the path.

Description

Most will experience some level of adversity at some point early in their lives. Those that are able to not only overcome but leverage those experiences into positive growth will acquire the important skills needed to complete the next phase (e.g., grit, optimism, accountability, decision-making skills, etc.). Passion begins to grow here.

Phase 1: Equipping the Warrior

Must Contain:	Cannot Contain:
• Adversity event(s)	• Entitlement
• Acquire core skills/values	• Being closed minded
• Learn decision-making skills	• Unwilling to make sacrifices and necessary time/energy

Description

This next phase can span decades, even a lifetime. The skills and perspective acquired in Phase 1 allow for the beginning of ideas, discovery of passion, and ability to move forward through this difficult phase. Allow yourself the time and space to think, if you want to begin to forecast, what may be coming on the horizon. This will be your opportunity.

Phase 2: Idea/Passion Generator

Must Contain:	Cannot Contain:
• Risk, sacrifice, work	• Indecision
• Forecasting of future	• Excessive amounts of distraction
• Time/space/lots of ideas and practice	• Lack of motivation
• Sustained persistence	• Complacency

Description

Timing is key. Be ready to take action. All your hard work, sacrifices, and ability to be comfortable with instability and change have given you this opportunity. The time will come to share your ideas and passion and change the world forever. This is your moment of impact; don't let it pass you by. Believe in yourself, and so will the world.

Phase 3: Moment of Impact

Must Contain:	Cannot Contain:
• Timing/urgency	• Being content/settling
• Willingness to share	• Concern of what others think
• Ignore naysayers	• Doubt of relevance
• Self-belief/internal motivation/mastery	• Doubt in success

Outcome

It is impossible to make a difference if you don't try. This book is about you, a young athlete, but you are different than most. A section wouldn't be included on how to change the world if I didn't believe you were capable of doing it. Be ready. Take action. Do it with integrity.

Regardless of what you choose to or our how you choose to do it, you've got to do it with a certain level of enthusiasm that inspires others to believe in it as much as you do.

Example of Effective Enthusiasm: In the Hutong district on Beijing, there lives a man named Mr. Liu. He has been recognized in various mainstream publications as the "cricket whisperer." He raises and trains crickets, some for fighting and some for carrying around in gourds to listen to during the long winter. I've never met anyone more enthusiastic about anything in my entire life. I left wanting to go home and find crickets to train. His enthusiasm for crickets was inspiring. Learn to unleash enthusiasm wisely. It's contagious—especially if it's not your normal personality.

> **"Nothing great was ever accomplished without enthusiasm."**
> —Ralph Waldo Emerson

Changing the world won't be easy, but don't be discouraged. The reality is that in your time spent on Earth, if you impact the life of only one other, you will have made a difference.

Tip: Don't worry about helping everyone all at once or helping everyone you want to pay it forward for in one day in the exact amount you hope. Just start somewhere, with something small; you never know what ripple effect one small extension of kindness might make.

It's common to hear about professional athletes who struggle with the transition of their days as athletes coming to end and what comes after. We hear about these stories because they're famous. The truth is, this is happening everywhere, all the time, to athletes like you and me. The truth is we should be ready; it's a transition we all know is coming and is a great opportunity to use all the skills and experiences we acquired during our time as athletes.

As you move through your journey as a young athlete, remember that your stats, GPA, and the college you attended are going to matter less and less. Instead what will be important is what you stand for, how you got there, if you can think, solve problems, are respectful to others, and have good judgment. This is your path, never been traveled, never to be traveled again. Make it count.

Todd Mann is no longer around, but a lot of what made him great can be found in today's young athletes like you—a combination of a good work ethic, a big heart, humility, and a quest to be both the best athlete and help others along the way while doing it. Being an athlete is fun and an important chapter of your life, but it will only be one chapter of many. If you've gotten this far in the book, it means you're not afraid of putting in the work in pursuit of using your time as an athlete to do good things for your journey and the journey of others.

The next chapter looks at the next phase of what the TM22 symbol represents and, if you're willing, what role you could play in making a difference together.

CONCLUSION: TM22 PART II

When I was just an eight-year-old kid and first met Todd Mann, I wasn't in a position to give back to young athletes; I was just starting to become one. In the years that followed, Todd would give me a lot, from his time to his advice to my first wood bat. But his most valuable gift may have been the example of how powerful it can be to help a young athlete on his or her own quest.

I've often thought about what I would say if I got the chance to tell Todd thank you for all he did for me. The truth is, he wouldn't want it. He would say that he did it because it was the right thing to do, not because he wanted to be thanked. He would have also said to just make sure that someday when I had the chance to help a young athlete, do the same. TM22 Part I talked about how this symbol came to be. Part II will explain what this symbol intends to become.

If even one athlete does their best to choose a path of integrity, stands up for principles important to them and their families, and helps other athletes along their path to reaching their maximum potential, it would be something Todd would be proud of, but together we can do a lot of good.

What is TM22?

A Man...
TM22 is the mark left by a baseball player, father, coach, friend, and mentor. It is a reminder of the man he was, the principles he stood for, and the power of helping other athletes achieve their goals. Don't underestimate the power of believing in someone, even before they do.

A Symbol...
TM22 is a symbol that represents the power of integrity, working hard, being accountable, having no regrets, and the willingness to give back and help others along their paths. This will be a symbol that reminds all of us, regardless of role, what it is we are working toward.

TM22 = Character + Integrity + Resilience

Character—Your character is your values shown through your actions. This is something you have control of regardless of background, money, gender, or ethnicity. It's what people will remember, and how it's defined is within your control.

Integrity—Integrity is showing your true character even when times are tough, being consistent, and doing the right thing even when no one is watching. If character is your values, integrity is living by them.

Resilience—If you are resilient, anything is possible. You must be able to overcome adversity and fight until you can fight no more. Sacrifice, persevere, and don't let anyone stop you.

Build character. *Show* integrity. *Develop* Resilience.

A Way of Life…
TM22 athletes aren't perfect, nor claim to be, but they do try their best to be themselves and make good decisions. Those who choose this lifestyle stand up for those in need, do what others aren't willing to do, earn every step along the way, and will work hard to build a definition of success created by themselves. TM22 is a symbol of being a successful young athlete but also a human on a quest to make a positive difference in the world. The skills acquired as a young athlete will allow this.

A Reminder…
This symbol is a reminder to say thank you to those who helped you along the way before it's too late. Show your gratitude and put into action the values that those who have helped you showed were important. This is the best way to "say" thank you.

A Team…
TM22 represents the alliance of current and former athletes, coaches, parents, teachers, and others who share the common goal of helping young athletes succeed. The best programs and athletes are those who were forced to work even harder because of their rivals. You can dislike each other, but the truth is that in the end, you need each other and are on a similar quest.

A Way of Thinking…
There are some athletes who refuse to be ordinary. They are willing to make the right choices and take the necessary actions needed to create the destiny of their choice. Your future is up to you to decide, and it will require a unique, brave, and resilient mindset. You have the tools.

A Connector...
Athletes need a neutral conduit that allows them to stay connected to one another. Together, athletes are stronger and need each other if reaching maximum potential really is a goal. The best interests of athletes and both the current and future paths will be taken care of and get the attention it deserves if athletes' band together, and we have the tools to create these links.

The Pillars of the TM22 Athlete Alliance: Equip. Empower. Excel.

Equip
The alliance aims to provide a variety of resources, tools, and support needed for athletes to reach their maximum potential as athletes and humans with integrity. We are trying to build a culture that equips athletes to pursue a culture of excellence with character through consistent intensity, focus, and passion. You have to choose to be excellent and need the right skills.

Empower
In order to make change lasting and genuine, our teaching style will follow a heuristic approach. We can provide knowledge, skills, resources, and encouragement, but we will also enable athletes to discover and learn for themselves. They must be responsible for creating their own path and be accountable for their actions. Building self-awareness, defining success, and providing a set of guiding principles will all be important parts of the alliance.

Excel
Success will be defined by growth, integrity shown through genuine action, and the ability to excel in life as well as in sports. Ongoing support and resources will be provided.

Increasing Access for Athletes: It will be critical to continue the discussion on moving the young-athlete paradigm forward and together build a future that is best for our athletes of any economic, gender, financial, cultural, and racial background. Ongoing research, scholarships, coach and athlete training, athlete mentorship program, parent discussions, athlete round tables, and an effective communication tool that links athletes to each other and new information are a few examples of these resources. For more information on opportunities and ways to work together, visit the TM22 website.

TM22athletes.com provides ongoing research, information, answers to frequently asked questions, and links to opportunities to continue to set yourself apart. This website is designed to connect athletes, coaches, and parents from around the world. It will continue to adapt, provide resources, and continue the discussion. This tool will allow us to move forward and give us the flexibility we need to adapt to a rapidly changing journey.

Example of TM22 in Action

In the spring of 2015, I wanted to test out some of the models I had been working on. I was coaching the intermediate baseball team at Punahou School, and it was the perfect group of players and parents. I've been a part of a lot of teams, both playing and coaching, in the previous ten-plus years with college athletes, and some were pretty good teams. This might have been my favorite group. The team had good athletes, but they worked hard, looked out for each other, and, for the most part, knew when to focus and when to be clowns. It made it really clear to me how important any sport at any level can be and how critical it is to create the environment for athletes to be able to earn what's given, empower them to take responsibility for their path, and equip them with skills they can apply beyond just a short two-month season. We didn't win every game in 2015 or the championship but it wasn't how success would be defined for that group. Building a foundation, developing habits, creating a culture and brotherhood that would continue during the years ahead were more important. This same group won the Intermediate championship the following year, the JV championship the next, and in 2019 won the state championship in Hawaii.

This team did have talent but they were also a hardworking, high character group. In 2019, for twenty-two consecutive Friday nights leading up to the start of their season, the members from the baseball program, ranging from intermediate to varsity, met at the hill near the top of our school. As a team, they ran over 10,100 hills, carrying everything from sandbags to rocks to tires to each other. They didn't run those hills for themselves, they ran them for each other.

In the Spring of 2020, their season and opportunity to repeat as state champs would be cut short, like athletes across the globe, due to the coronavirus. No one could have predicted this outcome, but after years of working hard, sacrificing, and understanding that you don't control outcomes, only the process, these athletes will leave with a brotherhood and no regrets.

Note: These athletes referred to their offseason workouts as TM22, but the credit for this shift in culture and accountability goes to the upperclassmen on the team; one of them was Jake. It was Jake who decided a change was needed in the program, and they were in pursuit of both character and a championship. In March of 2024, I watched Jake play for the University of Hawaii; he started in left field and went 3–5. Jake would be the first to tell you that, much like you, me, or Todd Mann, he's not perfect, but he is an example of what deciding to work hard and have integrity can do, not just for yourself but for those around you. I was proud to see Jake continuing to play and play well, but it's how he was treating his teammates, representing his last name, our school, and his community that matters and what people will remember. Don't underestimate the impact you can have on the culture that you're in, your ability to change, and deciding who you want to be.

There's a lot I would have told myself as an athlete, but maybe the most important is this: When people watch you play and continue to follow your path beyond the team they coached you on or the town you lived together in, it's not the outcome or stats they'll care about. It's the effort you showed, how you treat your teammates and coaches, and whether you respect the game. These are things you can control, and what now former athletes like me are looking for. It's easy for me to say now, but it's true, and it will last long after your days of being an athlete are over.

A Friend, Teammate, and Example of a TM22 Athlete: Darren Ginther

In late May of 2022, I made a last-minute trip to Minnesota to help my parents with some projects. One of my best friends, Darren Ginther, fit me into an early tee time at Phalen Golf Course in St. Paul before he headed out to a conference in Chicago. Darren was the director of the Office of College and Career Readiness for St. Paul Public Schools and oversaw school counselors in the state's second-largest school district.

I met Darren during my sophomore year of playing baseball at Augsburg College. We all knew from day one that "DG" was going to be good. He would go on to hold double-digit school records in baseball and may have been the greatest Auggie baseball player of all time.

On June 14th, a few weeks after our round of golf, Darren had a massive heart attack while exercising at home and would be taken off life support a few days later. His own father passed away from a heart attack when Darren was just eleven. Darren had a son and a daughter of his own.

Darren was an elite athlete. He excelled in baseball but also played football and competed in Olympic weightlifting in high school; he was also somehow a phenomenal bowler with pro form, and his most current dominance could be seen on the golf course. He was one of those people who really could do it all, but you would have never heard that from him or seen it in how he carried himself. He worked hard at being a good athlete and a good person, a true TM22 athlete.

At Darren's funeral and the services that followed, people spoke of his character, what he did to give back, and how he made others feel, and I don't remember any mention of statistics. His obituary in the *Star Tribune* was titled "He helped ensure success both in life and on the ballfield."

I'm writing this from the same table at the golf course where I last saw Darren, and I can't think of a better way to honor my good friend, my teammate, and my ally—DG.

> "Be a great ballplayer, but always be an even better dude."
> —Darren Ginther

Creating Your Own TM22 Culture

I haven't talked a lot about leadership in this book or how to be a good captain; those roles are important, but I think everyone can and should contribute. A leader is someone who identifies the needs of everyone in the group and does what they can to help them. They are not the loudest voice in the room, and you don't need a job title to lead and leave an impact. The best teams have a shared culture, a galvanizing symbol, and an aligned mission. TM22 can be that symbol, but it doesn't have to be. (If Todd Mann were still around, he'd probably laugh and tell you to do better.)

If you're in a position where you can influence the culture on your team and help those around you, do it. It will help you on your path too. Set the example, take the high road, don't be a front-runner, and try to create the environment where the magic described in this book can exist.

We've all had teammates who didn't really want to be there or were there just to socialize, and it can be hard at times if you're relying on them at any level to play a contributing role on the team. You can't force anyone to want it, but you can create the environment that may encourage them to get better, work harder, or at the very least, not be a cancer to the culture of the team.

Tip: **Leave Habits, Not Hazing.** Part of being a good captain, upperclassman, and leader is having a positive impact on athletes and a coach you may never know. If the younger kids in the program followed your lead on habits and culture, would the program and those athletes be in a better place? Don't underestimate how powerful it can be when a group of athletes decides they want to change things for the better. The impact of this can be felt for years to come, and most of the time this comes from a mindset shift from the players, not the coaches there at the time.

It took me twenty years to really understand what Todd Mann was doing for me and why. He was trying to help, but he knew the best way to do that was to just create the environment for me to able to work and earn, not just make my path easier. Letting me borrow his truck to get to my overnight shift at Brown Printing, linking me to the Herschman's to get the hardest job I've ever had doing masonry all summer, filling vending machines at our school while I did an independent study in the athletics office, opening the weight room, the list goes on, and I can't understate how impactful this environment was for me and how lucky I was to have it.

If you're in a position now to lead, as a captain, upperclassman, or just an athlete others respect, it's a huge opportunity to have an impact on a lot of people's lives. Take advantage of it. And when the day comes when you get asked to coach or have your own family, remember how powerful it can be to create this type of environment. Todd Mann was known for his willingness to pay it forward and help those around him.

What if the culture of your team needs improvement?

It happens. I see athletes get caught in the trap of rising up into programs known for being a certain way and then abandoning their own values to fit into that culture, even if it's a toxic one. Walking into a locker room as a freshman and telling the upperclassmen you're there to change the culture isn't going to go well, and you shouldn't do it, but you can start with your own actions. This is more important than what you say and needs to be done at practice, in class, at home, and when you don't think anyone is watching. Sometimes the best opportunity is rising up in a program known for being arrogant and leaving it as a program that people say, Wow, they're good athletes and great kids. You'd be surprised at how little it takes to change it, but you have to decide and hold people accountable. It can't just be show. Following and continuing a culture you know isn't good will be a regret. Sometimes connecting yourself to athletes outside your program can help cause a shift too, for example.

This book is about you, the athlete, and your journey, but we also all have a responsibility to steward this path for others. Not every athlete would care about this, but this book isn't designed for an ordinary athlete. Here's a way you can stay involved and leave a mark in your program.

The TM22 Athlete Alliance

The TM22 Athlete Alliance embodies Todd's giving spirit and hopes to enable athletes to work together. This alliance was built to help equip young athletes on their quest for greatness. Supported by the pillars and guided by core beliefs, the TM22 Athlete Alliance will help empower athletes from diverse backgrounds to form an alliance and achieve high levels of success on and off the field. More information about scholarships can be found online too.

If you'd like to get involved and hear what other athletes are saying, use the QR code to fill out a brief form that asks you a few questions about your current journey. The purpose of this is to keep a pulse on what's happening, provide up-to-date information, and make it accessible to athletes that need access now. This advice and data can be found at tm22athletes.com.

Conclusion

Over twenty-five years ago, an athlete went out of their way for another athlete. He believed in them and wanted them to reach their maximum potential as athletes and be equipped with skills that would help them reach their goals, whatever those were. This is what Todd Mann did for me.

Every athlete who reads this book will find themselves at different places along their journey as an athlete. This book was written to help you as an athlete, but being an athlete is just one component, one chapter of your life. The skills and lessons included in this book can help you in those other components and chapters as well. Remember that no act of kindness is too small, and you never know what people will remember. That is the legacy you want to leave behind. Don't underestimate yourself and your power to pay it forward. I hope someday, when you have the opportunity, you will do what you can to help another athlete on their journey.

Make the decision that you want more. Don't settle. Be willing to risk failure, and make the sacrifices needed to achieve greatness. Take action. Keep learning. Keep an open mind. Do whatever you can to set yourself apart. Enjoy the process. Refuse to be ordinary. Work hard. Be grateful. Be yourself. Be humble. Exceed expectations. Outwork everyone else. Make the sacrifices others aren't willing to make. Keep your integrity amid adversity, and people will remember your name. The path you're on right now matters, and it's worth all the sacrifices.

Greatness can be achieved by anyone willing to put in the work…so why not you?

Todd J. Mann
October 14, 1964–December 7, 2009

"Never let the fear of striking out prevent you
from playing the game."
—Babe Ruth

The Philosophy

Your trajectory is created by choice, not chance. If you don't like where you're headed or want something more, make the choice to change it. You are responsible for determining who you want to be and must take ownership of the path to get there.

The Pillars: Equip. Empower. Excel.

The Principles

1. TM22 athletes value integrity. They aren't choosing between reaching their maximum potential as athletes and leaving behind a legacy they're proud of—they are in pursuit of both.
2. TM22 athletes refuse to be ordinary. Hard work, sacrifices, and accountability are important to these athletes, and they are willing to show the sustained discipline needed to set themselves apart.
3. TM22 athletes belong to an alliance. These are athletes that care about more than just themselves and, when able, will seek ways to give back and make the path better for future athletes.

The Process

1. Make a Plan: The Power of Forecasting
2. Learn to Finish the Things That Matter
3. Sustain Self-Discipline and Self-Motivation
4. Seek Ways to Set Yourself Apart
5. Moments of Impact: Identify and Embrace
6. Surround Yourself with the *Right* People
7. Learn the Art of Risk-Taking
8. Build Perspective and Protect It
9. Form an Alliance with Adversity
10. Know Your Job. Be All In.
11. Develop Dynamic Balance
12. Give Back. Pay it Forward.
13. Enjoy the Process
14. If You Want to Be Anything, Timing is Everything
15. Improve Your Input; Improve Your Output
16. Unleash the Power of Sacrifice
17. True Confidence: Find It, Grow It, Share It
18. Show Character through *Genuine* Action
19. Invest Wisely with Your Time and Energy
20. Take Ownership of Your Own Development
21. Become a Master of Preparation
22. Outwork Everyone Else

Built by Athletes. For Athletes.

AFTERWORD

I was born in a small town called Waseca, Minnesota, in the first half of the 1980s. My mom worked at the public library, and my dad was a professor at the University of Minnesota-Waseca (UMW). I spent much of my early years running up and down the halls of the college with my cat Puff and watching the UMW Rams play in whichever sport was in season.

I only owned one key for much of my childhood. It wasn't a house key; we never locked the doors, and it wasn't to my bike because I never worried about anyone taking it. It was a key to turn on the tall stadium lights at Clear Lake Park for the occasional pick-up night game. This was important as our shortage was never of kids that wanted to play, only the amount of daylight. Our family never had a lot of money, but at home I had animals to take care of, a lawn to mow, food in the refrigerator, a dad that would play catch with me, a mom that took care of me, and an older sister to annoy. I had a running tab at Sportsman's Stop for snacks, bait, and renting video games. There were nearby forests with trees to climb and build forts in, cornfields to run through, and night skies full of stars to gaze at.

We had two lakes in town only a short bike ride away. In the summer, we would go fishing, swimming, eat Grandma Marilyn's stale Oreos, and watch the fireworks over Maplewood Park in July. We even had a boat to use, made of wood, two pontoons, and an old-school nautical steering wheel emerging from the floor. We got towed back to the dock more times than we returned on our own. Winters were cold but worth it, as this transformed our lakes into a place for ice fishing, hills for sledding, and outdoor hockey rinks for anyone to use.

The holidays were special. In December, neighborhoods would transform into wonderlands of snowmen and Christmas lights; on Halloween, trick-or-treating was city wide, safe, and encouraged; and in late June, the county fair would bring people from far and wide for good food, rides, and demolition derbies. The streets of Waseca were always relatively calm, except for the occasional parade that featured high school marching bands from around the area, Clydesdales, clowns in small cars, homecoming queens, and the high school sports teams throwing candy from floats. Regardless of the season, high school sporting events never seemed to fail to pack a gymnasium. It seemed as if the entire town would come and support the teams and the players, regardless of whether their kids were on the team. People were proud to have school spirit. The older kids knew the names of the younger kids, including me. It was common to know all your neighbors, both young and old, and there were very few fences in town.

The family of one of my best friends, Brock, was involved with real estate. His dad and uncles coached us for many summers, which had a significant impact on my childhood. (Grandma Marilyn with the house near the lake and stale Oreos was also Brock's grandma.). One summer they purchased or rented an old, abandoned church next to my house near Hartley Elementary. There wasn't anything inside and not room for much, except it was the perfect size for a full-sized batting cage—thus creating what we called "Baseball Heaven." No pews, just the cage, net, a home plate, and pitching machine sat on top of the steps, right where a pastor once preached. We had an automatic feeder set up, so balls would just magically keep coming. This old-fashioned feeder made it sometimes dangerous, unpredictable, and always fun. The balls appeared out of nowhere; it was as if Jesus himself were throwing us batting practice.

There were older kids to look up to and younger kids to watch over; it really was the ideal habitat for a growing young athlete. It was a bubble in some ways but also important to note that it was just a short trip up the Snake Trail from seeing Kirby Puckett hit bombs for the Minnesota Twins in the Hubert H. Humphrey Metrodome in Minneapolis. My favorite team, the Minnesota Twins, won the World Series in 1987 and 1991. The Twins haven't been back since. It really couldn't get any better. I was growing, and so were my dreams. The story I'm sharing sounds made up, and I understand now how incredibly lucky I was to even have one component of this bubble. But like most bubbles, it would eventually burst.

On April 6, 2016, the grandstand, clubhouse, and concession stand at Tink Larson Field burned to the ground. First built in the late 1930s as part of President Franklin D. Roosevelt's Works Progress Administration, this was a second home to many…including me.

My journey as a young athlete began here—shagging baseballs and then batboy, buying popcorn from Sharon at the concession stand, becoming friends with Todd Mann, and then playing baseball here for over a decade. Tink Larson, for whom the field is named, has coached and maintained not only the field but the sport of baseball in Waseca, Minnesota, for nearly half a century. Rain or shine, for all but a few of those years, he was the only one to ever rake the mound and cut the grass. Days after the fire, Coach Larson would say this was the second worst day of his life, the death of his wife Sharon a few years prior being the worst. Hundreds of community members watched the fire that spring night. Even in turmoil, that structure knew how to bring people together. The community is strong; the grandstand was rebuilt; it's not the same, but perhaps that's ok. The locker that Todd built for me in his garage many summers ago is gone, but the memories and bond the brotherhood of men built together those hot summer nights will never be lost.

Coach Larson had lost his best friend Todd Mann, his wife Sharon, and now his field. It's been over twenty years since I last played for Coach Larson at his field, but he continues to teach me valuable lessons. He continues to lead by genuine action on how to overcome adversity, hasn't allowed for others or himself to feel sorry for him, and no matter what, he will keep moving forward. Coach Larson not only taught me how to play baseball, but he also showed me how to become a good man.

In June of 2016, I drove down to Waseca to visit coach. I met him at his house, and after we adjusted the sprinklers on the baseball field, we went into his office. After nearly fifty years of being a successful teacher, athletic director, and coach, his walls are now covered in Hall of Fame awards, accolades, and trophies. However, it is clear that his most treasured items are those of his late wife Sharon, his best friend Todd Mann, his 1990 state championship team, and pictures with his sons, Mike and Paul. We talked for a few hours that morning about sports, life, good memories, and the current challenges we saw for today's young athletes and how they have changed over the years. As I left that day, Coach Larson walked me out to my car, and I had a chance to say thank you—something I never did with Todd Mann before he passed. After I thanked him, he put his hand on my shoulder, looked me in the eye, and smiled just as he did when I was eight years old. I will never forget it.

It wasn't until I drove out of town that day that I realized how fortunate I was to have had the young-athlete experience that I did. The University of Minnesota-Waseca where my dad once worked is now a prison; the church we used to take batting practice from God in has been torn down; the grandstand at Tink Larson Field burned to the ground; my favorite umpire, Charlie Fuller, and my friend's grandma, Marilyn, have passed away; the lights we had the key to at Clear Lake Park are no longer there; and only a few of my teammates remain in town. It is still a great town and always my home, but the early '90s version of Waseca, Minnesota, is a thing of the past. I have to remind myself that it is unrealistic to think that we can try to create this kind of atmosphere for every athlete—probably not even my own child. The good news is that the most important things here can't be burned down, and we can make it possible for every kid.

What I really treasured about my childhood weren't the buildings, but that I always felt like people cared about me. I felt safe. I mattered. I felt as if anything was possible, and there were people willing to help me reach my dreams. There was a community of people that, regardless of differences, was still a community. No one can ever take away the memories and person it enabled me to become. So, while buildings don't last forever, the memories of those who walked with us on our path can. This is the power of youth athletics, the impact of doing things the right way, and an example of why this path in life can be so important. I hope you will join me in creating a community that supports our athletes both now and for the young athletes they may one day raise themselves.

ACKNOWLEDGMENTS AND GRATITUDE

Thank you to my teammates, the coaches and teachers who believed in me, and to all the people who have contributed to my quest. You have enabled the path I am on today.

To my family: My dad for playing catch with me countless summer nights after long days at work and never complaining, for being a mentor and father, and for all the sacrifices you have made for our family throughout the years, both seen and unseen. My mom for being the toughest member of our family, for creating and holding down the homestead, and for being the voice of reason and consistent positive support. My sister for showing me the power of toughness, endurance, and humility. You all continue to make sacrifices for me, and I'm forever grateful.

To Waseca, Minnesota: For the great people, harsh weather, and everything a young athlete needed to grow and feel encouraged to chase their dreams. You will always be home.

Maverick, Blue, Su, and Shelby: I am proud to be a part of our flock. Thank you for sticking with me through the ups and downs of this project and inspiring me to keep going.

The Nelsons (Blain, Blake, Blair): Although we are not related, you treated me like a son. Thank you for creating "Baseball Heaven," long practices on WHS Field 2, picking me up for morning runs on the Hartley track, and for being great role models to your kids and to so many young men.

Tink Larson: You made me love the game of baseball. I wanted nothing more than to make you proud, and you are and will always be the best coach I ever had. Thank you for welcoming me into the clubhouse, into the dugout, and into a brotherhood that changed my life.

Adam Christ and Nick Rathmann: Every young athlete needs older kids to look up to; you were some of those guys. Thank you for being hard on me, including me on long road trips, and for showing me the power that having positive mentors around young athletes can have.

Mike Walker: Thank you for taking a chance on me. You enabled my entrance into the world of teaching and taught me the importance of sound decision-making, brain research, and the power of doing what you believe is right even when difficult.

4-Seasons Athletics: Cindy and Jane, thank you for allowing me to be a part of the 4-Seasons, Piche, Bartelt, and 4-Seasons family. Your sons had a big impact on me, and I'm proud to be on your team. It was the perfect environment for a kid like me, and I am still honored to be a part of it.

Jay Asmus and the Minneapolis Angels: I think often of our times spent on the field and parking lots. I wish every athlete had that type of postcollege-career playing environment where competition, laughter, and brotherhood could continue. Thanks for creating that environment and welcoming DG and me.

Darren Ginther: You were the best teammate, friend, father, and ally. Your belief in me was sincere, and we all miss you.

Punahou School: Thank you for your support and trust and for allowing me to work with so many great students, teachers, and families.

Hawaii Pacific University: Coach Yukumoto, you took a chance on a kid from Minnesota. Thank you. Coach Les, you taught me the importance of teaching life lessons through sports and welcomed me into your family. And to all the Sea Warriors I coached, I will never forget all the 6:30 a.m. weights, van rides to Ke'ehi Lagoon, runs to UPS, hours in the library basement, and battles we went through together on the field. Thank you for making me a part of your 'ohana.

Augsburg College: You gave me an opportunity, pushed me when I needed it, and created an environment to grow as an athlete and person. I will always be proud to be an Auggie. Coach Bateman, thank you for visiting me in the hospital and giving me the opportunity to start my coaching career. Missy Strauch, trainer and good friend, thank you for all your sacrifices and for helping so many young athletes like me along the way when they needed it most.

Pastor Dave Wold: You created a safe environment for me to listen, learn, and think. You taught me the power of remembering people's names and are an example of integrity in action.

The 2015 Punahou Intermediate Gold Baseball Team: Thank you for reminding me what it's all about to be a young athlete and why this path is so important.

To Todd Mann, #22: You believed in me before I did, and you didn't judge me by who I was but by who you thought I could become. My hope is that other young athletes will benefit the same amount from the inspiration and lessons you have given me.

To the Athlete Reading This Book: Thank you for taking the time to read this book. All the time, struggles, sacrifices, and energy put in will be worth it. Don't ever forget the perspective you have now as a young athlete, and find a way to pay it forward someday when you have the chance.

ABOUT THE AUTHOR

Andy Nelson grew up in southern Minnesota. Football, hockey, baseball, and fishing with friends filled much of his childhood. After high school, Nelson chose to attend Augsburg College, a Division III school located in Minneapolis, Minnesota, where he would play middle infield for the Auggies from 2003–2007 (medical redshirt 2006). Nelson collected a few accolades along the way, but he is most proud of being awarded the Darrell Weisse Most Respected Player Award in his senior year. Coach Weisse was a great guy, a mentor, and the reason Andy attended Augsburg College. After graduating, Nelson remained at Augsburg College as an assistant coach in addition to running summer strength-and-conditioning hockey programs and individual instruction at Acceleration Northwest in Plymouth, Minnesota.

In 2008, Nelson worked for Ripken Baseball on the "Ripken Road Show," assisting with clinics across the southeastern United States. This unique model allowed him to work with coaches, players, parents, and other Ripken instructors from across the United

States. The next path would lead to Hawaii, where he was offered a graduate assistant position at Hawaii Pacific University. At this Division II school, Nelson was the strength/conditioning and infield coach and helped play a role in the Sea Warriors completing their best season in school history in 2009–2010. He coached at HPU as an assistant and was the head coach of a summer collegiate team in the Paradise League for three years. After Nelson graduated with a master's degree in global leadership and sustainable development, his passion for helping other athletes remained, and he soon became involved at a local school.

In 2011, Nelson began working at Punahou School. Located on the island of Oahu, Punahou is one of the largest, single campus independent schools in the nation with an enrollment of nearly four thousand students. Throughout the year, Nelson is tasked with facilitating over one thousand students on overnight excursions across the islands and coordinating the activities within the outdoor education progression. This unique position allows for collaboration with a wide spectrum of parents, teachers, and students K–12. Nelson is now the K–12 Director of Outdoor Education, and the program continues to grow.

The lives of athletes have never been more complicated. Nelson is continuing to try to find ways to support the evolution of the lives of young athletes to make sure they are equipped, empowered, and encouraged that the path they are on matters. The TM22 Athlete Alliance was built to enable ongoing resources and support for young athletes on a quest for greatness, on and off the field. For more information about the 22 Guide, the TM22 program, resources, contact information, and access to ongoing research, please visit the TM22 website. (tm22athletes.com).

REFERENCES AND ADDITIONAL RESOURCES

Aurelius, Marcus, and Gregory Hays. *Meditations.* New York: Modern Library, 2002. Print.

Bellwood Rewinds. Electric Motor and Diesel Generator Experts www.bellwoodrewinds.co.uk

Brackett, Marc A. *Permission to Feel: Unlocking the Power of Emotions to Help Our Kids, Ourselves, and Our Society Thrive.* Celadon Books, 2019. Print.

Brand, Stewart. *The Clock of the Long Now: Time and Responsibility.* New York: Basic, 1999. Print.

Brockman, John. *Thinking: The New Science of Decision-Making, Problem-Solving, and Prediction.* Harper Perennial, 2013. Print.

Brooks, David. *The Road to Character.* New York: Random House, 2015. Print.

Bush, Ryan A. *Designing the Mind: The Principles of Psychitecture.* Designing the Mind, 2021.

Campbell, Jeremy. *Winston Churchill's Afternoon Nap: A Wide-Awake Inquiry into the Human Nature of Time.* New York: Simon and Schuster, 1986. Print.

Cambridge Free English Dictionary and Thesaurus. *Cambridge Free English Dictionary and Thesaurus.* Web. 7 Sept. 2015. https://dictionary.cambridge.org/

Carchia, Carl. & Kelley, Bruce. *"Hey data – Swing!"* July 16, 2013. http://espn.go.com/espn/story/_/id/9469252/hidden-demographics-youth-sports-espn-magazine

Chopra, Sanjiv, and David Fisher. *Leadership by Example: The Ten Key Principles of All Great Leaders.* New York: Thomas Dunne, 2012. Print.

Clear, James. *Atomic Habits: An Easy & Proven Way to Build Good Habits & Break Bad Ones: Tiny Changes, Remarkable Results.* Avery, an Imprint of Penguin Random House, 2018. Print.

Coyle, Daniel. *The Culture Code: The Secrets of Highly Successful Groups.* Bantam Books. Random House US, 2018.

Dalio, Ray. *Principles.* Simon & Schuster, 2017. Print.

Dictionary, Encyclopedia and Thesaurus. *The Free Dictionary.* Farlex. Web. 31 May 2016.

Does Youth Sports get the Math all Wrong? Changing the Game Project. http://changingthegameproject.com/does-youth-sports-get-the-math-all-wrong/

Dweck, Carol S. *Mindset: The New Psychology of Success.* New York: Random House, 2006. Print.

Durant, Will. *The Story of Philosophy: The Lives and Opinions of the Greatest Philosophers.* Simon & Schuster, 1926.

Eiseley, Loren C. *The Immense Journey. An Imaginative Naturalist Explores the Mysteries of Man and Nature.* Alexandria, VA, Time-Life Books, 1981.

Epstein, David. *The Sports Gene: Inside the Science of Extraordinary Athletic Performance.* Turtleback Books, 2014.

Fitzhenry, Robert I. *The Harper Book of Quotations.* 3rd ed. New York: Harper Perennial, 1993. Print.

Frank, Laurie S. *Journey Toward the Caring Classroom: Using Adventure to Create Community in the Classroom & Beyond*. Oklahoma City, OK: Wood 'N' Barnes, 2004. Print.

Frankl, Viktor E. *Man's Search for Meaning*. Boston: Beacon Press, 1962.

Gallaher, John G. *General Alexandre Dumas: Soldier of the French Revolution*. Carbondale: Southern Illinois UP, 1997. Print.

Gallo, Carmine. *The Storyteller's Secret: From TED Speakers to Business Legends, Why Some Ideas Catch on and Others Don't*. New York: St. Martins, 2016. Print.

Gladwell, Malcolm. *Outliers: The Story of Success*. New York: Little, Brown, 2008. Print.

Greene, Robert. *The Daily Laws: 366 Meditations on Power, Seduction, Mastery, Strategy and Human Nature*. Profile Books, 2021.

Greene, Robert. *Mastery*. New York: Penguin Books, 2012. Print.

Greene, Robert. *The Laws of Human Nature*. Penguin USA, 2019. Print.

Guillebeau, Chris. *Happiness of Pursuit*. New York: Harmony, 2014. Print.

Harman, Willis W. *An Incomplete Guide to the Future*. San Francisco: San Francisco Book; 1976. Print.

Holtz, Lou. *Winning Every Day: The Game Plan for Success*. New York: Harper Business, 1998. Print.

Jeter, Derek, and Jack Curry. *The Life You Imagine: Life Lessons for Achieving Your Dreams*. New York: Crown, 2000. Print.

Johnson, Michael. *Slaying the Dragon: How to Turn Your Small Steps to Great Feats*. New York: Regan, 1996. Print.

Kahneman, Daniel. *Thinking, Fast and Slow*. New York: Farrar, Straus, and Giroux, 2013. Print.

Keller, Gary, and Jay Papasan. *The One Thing: The Surprisingly Simple Truth behind Extraordinary Results*. Austin, TX: Bard, 2012. Print.

Kelly, Matthew. *Off Balance: Getting beyond the Work-Life Balance Myth* to *Personal and Professional Satisfaction.* Beacon Printing, 2015. Print.

Krogerus, Mikael, and Roman Tschappeler. *The Decision Book: Fifty Models for Strategic Thinking.* New York: W.W. Norton, 2012. Print.

Lahey, Jessica. *The Gift of Failure: How the Best Parents Learn to Let Go so Their Children Can Succeed.* 2015. Print.

Leavell, Kate. Meet in the Middle, salvaging our youth sports experience. March 5, 2016. http://kateleavell.com/2016/03/05/meet-in-the-middle-salvaging-our-youth-sports-experience/

Lesyk, Jack J. Ph.D. The Nine Mental Skills of Successful Athletes. https://www.sportpsych.org/nine-mental-skills-overview

Liebenberg, Louis. *The Art of Tracking: The Origin of Science.* David Philip, 2001.

Loehr, James E. *The New Toughness Training for Sports: Mental, Emotional, and Physical Conditioning from One of the World's Premier Sports Psychologists.* Plume, 1995.

Lonetree, Anthony. *He helped ensure success both in life and on the ballfield.* Star Tribune. Friday, July 8, 2022. Print.

Luckner, John L., and Nadler, Reldan S. *Processing the Experience: Strategies to Enhance and Generalize Learning.* Dubuque, IA: Kendall/Hunt, 1997. Print.

Mack, Gary, and David Casstevens. *Mind Gym: An Athlete's Guide to Inner Excellence.* New York: Contemporary, 2001. Print.

Marchant, Jo. *Cure: A Journey into the Science of Mind over Body.* New York: Crown Publishers. 2016. Print.

Matheny, Mike, and Jerry B. Jenkins. *The Matheny Manifesto: A Young Manager's Old School Views on Success in Sports and Life.* Print.

Maurer, Robert. *One Small Step Can Change Your Life: The Kaizen Way.* New York: Workman, 2004. Print.

Maxwell, John C. *Thinking for a Change: 11 Ways Highly Successful People Approach Life and Work.* New York: Warner, 2003. Print.

McRaven, William H. *Make your bed little things that can change your life…and maybe the world.* New York: Grand Central Publishing, 2017. Print.

McCready, Amy. *The Me, Me, Me Epidemic: A Step-by-step Guide to Raising Capable, Grateful Kids in an Over-entitled World.* Print.

Millman, Dan. *Body Mind Mastery: Creating Success in Sport and Life.* Rev. ed. Novato, Calif.: New World Library: 1999. Print.

Mlodinow, Leonard. *The Upright Thinkers: The Human Journey from Living in Trees to Understanding the Cosmos.* New York: Vintage, 2015. Print.

Nelson, Eric M. *Cultivating outdoor classrooms: designing and implementing child-centered learning environments.* St. Paul, MN: Redleaf Press, 2012. Print.

Nightingale, Earl. *The Strangest Secret.* www.bnpublishing.com, 2007.

Orlick, Terry. *In Pursuit of Excellence: How to Win in Sport and Life through Mental Training.* 2nd ed. Champaign, IL: Leisure, 1990. Print.

O'Sullivan, John. *Changing the Game: The Parent's Guide to Raising Happy, High-performing Athletes and Giving Youth Sports Back to Our Kids.* Print.

Potter, Beverly A. *The way of the Ronin: a guide to career strategy.* New York, NY, AMACOM, 1984.

Ralph Waldo Emerson Texts. Self-Reliance by Ralph Waldo Emerson. Essay. http://www.emersoncentral.com/selfreliance.htm

Ripken, Cal, and Bill Ripken. *Play Baseball the Ripken Way: The Complete Illustrated Guide to the Fundamentals.* New York: Random House, 2004. Print.

Schopp, Claude. *Alexandre Dumas: Genius of Life.* New York: Franklin Watts, 1988. Print.

Siewert, C.J. Waseca's *Tink Larson: A Class Act and One-Of-A-Kind Baseball Legend*. June 13, 2012. http://www.mnbaseball.org/News/370

Tough, Paul. *How Children Succeed: Grit, Curiosity, and the Hidden Power of Character*. Print.

Trump, Miles. *Caretaker of the field: Waseca's Larson maintains Tink Larson Field for more than 4 decades*. Waseca County News. Jul 3, 2013 http://www.southernminn.com/waseca_county_news/sports/local/article_d6c44bde-47e4-53a1-b6d9-65155a8e4671.html

VanDeWeghe, Kiki and DiFiori, John. Special for *USA Today* Sports. *Kids should play multiple sports and not just focus on one*. http://www.usatoday.com/story/sports/nba/2015/08/13/children-sports-skill-development/31680375/

Wagner, Tony, and Ted Dintersmith. *Most likely to succeed: preparing our kids for the innovation era*. New York, NY, Scribner, 2016.

Warren, William E. *Coaching and Motivation: A Practical Guide to Maximum Athletic Performance*. Englewood Cliffs, N.J.: Prentice-Hall, 1983. Print.

Webster's Biographical Dictionary. Springfield, Mass.: G. & C. Merriam, 1980. Print.

Wilson, Edward O. *The meaning of human existence*. Liveright Publishing Corporation, a division of W.W. Norton & Company, 2015.

Wimbrow, Dale. *The Man in the Glass*. c1934 1895-1954 – Updated Version.

Wooden, John, and Steve Jamison. *Wooden on Leadership*. New York: McGraw-Hill, 2005. Print.

Zeldin, Theodore. *The Hidden Pleasures of Life*. 2015, Page 27.

Ziglar, Zig, and Zig Ziglar. *See You at the Top*. Gretna: Pelican Pub. 1979. Print.

www.ingramcontent.com/pod-product-compliance
Lightning Source LLC
LaVergne TN
LVHW020926090426
835512LV00020B/3220